WILDLIFE
FOLKLORE

by

Laura C. Martin

Illustrations by Mauro Magellan

The
Globe
Pequot
Press

Old Saybrook, Connecticut

Copyright © 1994 by Laura C. Martin

Cover and text illustrations by Mauro Magellan
Cover and book design by Nancy Freeborn

Library of Congress Cataloging-in-Publication Data
Martin, Laura C.
    Wildlife folklore / by Laura C. Martin : illustrations by
Mauro Magellan. — 1st ed.
    182 p. ; cm. ill.
    ISBN 1-56440-499-4
    ISBN 1-56440-974-0 (PBK)
    1. Animals—Folklore. 2. Insects—Folklore. I. Title.
GR705.M37 1994
398.24'52—dc20   94-21560
                                                          CIP

Manufactured in the United States of America
First Edition/Third Printing

To my friend Sally McMillan

ACKNOWLEDGMENTS

Thanks goes to my children, David and Cameron, for their patience
and understanding, to my parents, Ken and Lois Coogle, for instilling within me a love of nature at an early age, and to Bill Brenner for
his unwavering support and encouragement.

CONTENTS

MAMMALS

INSECTS AND ARACHNIDS

REPTILES AND AMPHIBIANS

PREFACE

I was seven years old when I was bitten by a wolf, an event that made a lasting impression on my young life. I was, among my friends, the only one who had been bitten by a wolf, and I loved the distinction, imagining myself to have been touched by the wild. I never tired of telling the tale, and over the years the story grew until I gradually began omitting a few unessential parts, like the fact that the wolf was a pet and on a leash when he bit me, and that the bite itself was a tiny wound, leaving a scar only two inches across.

No matter how tame the circumstances, though, from the moment his teeth touched my leg, I considered the wolf to be my special animal. If I had grown up in a different time, in a different culture, the wolf would have been declared my spirit animal, and I would have been encouraged to study wolves closely and to learn what their wild spirit could teach me. But as a child of the twentieth century, my early connection with the wolf was seen as nothing more than a freak accident, and I was allowed to choose my own path and my own work.

The ways of nature are strange and wonderful, though, and here I am, decades later, studying wolves and bears and bats and beavers, learning from them and communicating to you the importance of the wild animals in our cultural history. We all have much to learn from these wild animals, and it is my hope that you, too, will be touched by the wild.

INTRODUCTION

*"In the beginning of all things, wisdom and knowledge were with the animals;
for Tirawa, the One Above, did not speak directly to man. He sent certain animals
to tell men that he showed himself through the beasts, and that from them,
and from the stars and the sun and the moon, man should learn."*

—Chief Letakots-Lesa of the Pawnee Tribe

From centuries-old oral epics to modern allegories, animals play a primary role in the myths, legends, and religious stories of every culture.
Animals were the first neighbors of humans in the prehistoric world,
where food was scarce and danger abundant. Humans were weak, hairless,
shortsighted, and slow—conditions that made their existence in this time pre-
carious. Animals were the early humans' first teachers. They watched them
respectfully, observed them carefully, and learned from them quickly.

Early hunting cultures, in fact, were completely dependent on animals for
their survival. If game was plentiful and the hunter successful, the people survived. If the animals disappeared, or if the hunters were unable to kill them,
the people died of starvation. Because their lives were so closely entwined
with those of the animals, early humans held great respect for the animals
they hunted. As humans developed myths to explain the mysteries of their
existence, they very often incorporated the animals into their system of
beliefs, seeing them as messengers of gods or sometimes as gods themselves.

The hunt, then, became a paradox. The animals, which the humans
respected and even worshipped, had to be killed for food, and with the killing
came guilt at taking the animal's life and fear that the animals would disappear
and the people would go hungry. In an attempt to lessen their guilt, and in
the hopes of appeasing the animals' spirits, our ancestors developed rites and
ceremonies that showed their reverence for these animals. When Inuits killed
a polar bear, for example, a celebration was held during which the hunters fed
the entire village for four days. After the festivities, the bear's skull was ceremoniously placed in a communal house, and gifts were offered to its spirit.

It was believed that if the spirit was pleased by these rites, the animals
would reappear to be sacrificed again and the tribe would have plenty to eat.

If the spirit of the animal was offended, however, the animals would disappear and the people would starve.

Joseph Campbell, author of numerous books on myth and folklore, says that the basic hunting myth was a covenant between animals and humans. Animals sacrificed their lives willingly, and humans, through ceremony and rites, returned the animal's spirit to the soil, the mother, to be born again. Proof of these early rituals lies in caves high in the Alps, where Neanderthal shrines filled with the skulls of the cave bear have been found. Participation in these rituals provided humans with a methodology for allowing the mind and spirit to deal with the questions of death and immortality.

Myths also helped humans to explain the question of the origin of the world. Creation myths are an integral part of the mythology of every culture. The stories vary in context and imagery, with the primary characters and setting reflecting the civilizations from which the stories developed. In spite of the differences in these stories, every myth about the creation of the world portrays the central theme of the many coming from the One.

Among North American Indians, stories of creation belong to a remote mythical age before the dawn of mankind. In the stories, the world is occupied by bird and animal spirits in human forms.

The Mythical Age was followed by what is referred to as the Age of Transformation, during which various animals changed the world to what it is today. Myths from this period explain how various animals were created and how they received characteristic marks (as how the chipmunk received its dark stripes), or how various natural landmarks were created. A transformation story from the North Pacific Coast area, for example, tells how Coyote created the Columbia River. One day Coyote jeered at tiny drops of water coming from the earth. The water became angry and chased Coyote, who ran and ran. When Coyote finally stopped to look behind him, he saw a great river following him. (The river later became known as the Columbia.)

Transformers such as the coyote are often called culture heroes. They are characters, both human and animal, who bring gifts to humankind. Culture-hero animals include the mink in the Pacific Northwest, the hare in the eastern woodlands, and the spider in the Southwest. Culture heroes are given credit for stealing fire, bringing the sun to earth, bringing corn, beans, and tobacco, and teaching humans about medicines and various ceremonies and rites.

The trickster hero is another common mythical character, often involved in amusing tales or stories that teach a moral. The trickster is usually portrayed as boastful and greedy, and the humor in these stories is sometimes lewd or obscene. The trickster hero often dies from his own stupidity, but the "death" is usually temporary, with the trickster claiming to have been asleep.

Animals have also played a large role in cultural traditions such as naming and initiation rites. In almost all North American Indian nations, for instance, the personal acquisition of a guardian spirit animal was strongly encouraged. Letakots-Lesa of the Pawnee wrote, "When a man sought to know how he should live, he went into solitude and cried until in vision some animal brought wisdom to him. It was Tirawa who sent his messages through the animals. . . . Thus were sacred songs and ceremonial dances given the Pawnees through the animals."

In a typical vision quest, a young man nearing puberty is sent into the wilderness alone and without food to fast until an animal spirit appears to him. Likewise, a girl at her first menses is sent to sit alone in a small house until she, too, sees the image of the animal that would serve as her guide.

Although this guardian spirit was thought to hold powers that would help the individual throughout a lifetime, the Oglala Sioux believed this spirit was sometimes not used until a person neared middle age. At this time in life, when the emphasis of a person's life shifts from the physical to the spiritual, the guardian animal was believed to help one make this change.

In addition, animals have been believed to be instrumental in curing illnesses, both directly, when various animal parts are used as medicine, and spiritually, when the powers of different animals are called upon to invoke a cure. Many Native American people believed that illness is caused when the balance of the world is disrupted. This balance, in which plants, animals, rocks, and humans are all equal, has to be restored before the human patient can recover. Curing ceremonies involved the entire community, both humans and animals.

Among the Zuni, the bear, badger, weasel, rattlesnake, and gopher figured predominantly in healing ceremonies. Among the Hopi, the bear was considered the most powerful doctor because he could dig deep into the earth and uncover important roots and medicines.

Shamans, the magic medicine men or women of the tribe, were thought to be able to take animal shapes to travel to the spirit world to effect a cure. The shamans were thought to be so powerful that they could cause, as well as cure, disease.

Whether the animals were seen as heroes or tricksters, their importance to the spiritual lives of our ancestors cannot be overemphasized. Because the essence of the soul cannot be divided, the soul of the animals was thought to be the same as the soul of humans, and it was believed that, upon the death of the body, a human soul often took the form of an animal, especially a winged animal that can flee the confines of earth and fly to the heavens.

Originating in Europe, the delusion that one could turn into a half-human/half-animal with the characteristics of a wolf was called *lycanthropy,* from the Greek word *lycos,* meaning "wolf." Werewolves are the most famous manifestation of this belief, although were-leopards and were-jaguars are often described in tales from Central and South America. In some cultures lycanthropy was thought to be hereditary. In others it was believed to be caused by enchantments and visions or by a bite from the animal.

Among the well-known examples of the role of animals in cultural traditions are the stories of the Greek slave Aesop. Devised around 600 B.C., Aesop's fables were composed both to teach and entertain, a purpose they accomplish to this day. Among the most famous of these fables are The City Mouse and the Country Mouse and The Fox and the Grapes. The first textbook on animals was written by the Greek philosopher Aristotle, in the fourth century B.C. The writings of the Roman scholar Pliny the Elder included thirty-seven volumes on natural history, four of which were zoology texts.

During the Middle Ages bestiaries became popular in Europe. In these books moral and ethical teachings are presented allegorically, using the characteristics of various animals to symbolize various sins or virtues. For example, the antelope with its two horns represents man armed with two weapons, the Old Testament and the New Testament. When the antelope catches its horns in the bushes, its predicament symbolizes humankind being caught by temptation.

From the fables of Aesop to the guardian animals of the Pawnee, animals have held an unquestionable influence on the development of human civilization. In the sophistication of the late twentieth century, what is the lesson that we can learn from animals today? Do the animals of the wild still influence us? Does our present knowledge of the natural history of these animals diminish their importance in our eyes? Does information result in respect or complacency?

In his book, *Way of the Animal Powers*, Joseph Campbell wrote:

"The animal envoys of the Unseen Power no longer serve, as in primeval times, to teach and to guide mankind. . . . Neither in body nor in mind do we inhabit the world of those hunting races of the Paleolithic millennia, to whose lives and life ways we nevertheless owe the very forms of our bodies and structures of our minds. Memories of their animal envoys still must sleep, somehow, within us; for they wake a little and stir when we venture into wilderness."

Many philosophers and psychologists have written about the First Mind, which includes all of our animal instincts, and the Second Mind, which includes our power to reason and sets us apart from the other animals. Although the Second Mind of humankind produces the glories of our civilizations—art, music, literature, technology, and medical science—the cry for the First Mind will not be silenced. The writings of Clarissa Estés, Robert Johnson, Sam Keen, and dozens of others warn us that separation from our First Mind, from our instincts, is resulting in the destruction of our earth and of our spirits. Perhaps it is time, once again, to learn from the wolf, the coyote, the elk, and the bear, to watch as they care for and protect their young and live in harmony with their environment.

No matter how carefully we have insulated our civilization from the wilderness and separated ourselves from the unpredictable vagaries of nature, we are still kin to the animals, superior in some ways, appallingly inferior in others, but in the end neither better nor worse than the creatures with whom we share this planet. When we shiver when a coyote howls in the distant darkness, when we gasp with pleasure as a mountain goat stands silhouetted against an impossibly blue sky, when we shudder as a poisonous snake crosses our path, and when we laugh at the antics of a squirrel gathering nuts for winter, it becomes clear that we are part of the natural world and that the spirit of the animals is the same as the spirit of humanity. We can believe, truly, that many came from One.

Note: The animals discussed in this volume are all indigenous to North America. The folklore found here, however, is based on myths and legends from cultures around the world and is not confined to the particular species that live in North America. For example, myths and superstitions about bats from Europe and the Orient are included along with folklore about species found only in North America.

MAMMALS

ANTELOPE

COMMON NAME: Antelope

SCIENTIFIC NAME: *Antilocapra americana*

DESCRIPTION: This deerlike creature stands 3 to 4 feet tall at the shoulder and is sandy brown with a white chest and belly and distinctive light bands on the neck and throat. The rump is white with hairs that stand erect when the animal is startled. Both males and females carry antlers, though the females' antlers are generally smaller.

HABITAT AND RANGE: Antelope make their home in open grasslands, prairies, and desert areas throughout the western part of the North American continent from southern Canada to northern Mexico.

Antelopes, also called pronghorns, are considered the fastest land animal in the United States. Antelopes are probably best remembered in the United States for their starring role in the American cowboy ballad, "Home, Home on the Range," in which the open prairie is glorified as the place where the deer and the antelope play. . . ."

Long before that lonesome song was penned, however, the antelope played roles in other cultures. In Roman mythology, the antelope is sacred to Minerva, the goddess of wisdom. In Egyptian mythology, antelopes are sacred to Isis and also sometimes represent Osiris and Horus. The appearance of the dog star, Sirius, in the east was once considered a portent that the Nile River would begin to rise and would irrigate the crops. It was thought that the antelope was always the first to see this star and would signal its presence by sneezing.

In Africa, Bushmen believed that the antelope alone could show one the way to the dwelling place of God. It was believed that God sometimes took the shape of an antelope. Even today, many African countries picture antelope on their coins.

The name antelope is from the Greek word *antholop*, which is formed from two words— *anthos*, meaning "flower," and *ops*, meaning "eye"—and refers to the beautiful eyes of the animal. Antelopes are closely related to the gazelle, about which there is much folklore. In the Far East the gazelle is considered a symbol of a gentle woman. The phrase *aine el lezozel*, meaning "you have the eyes of an antelope," is thought to be a high compliment.

A European medieval bestiary shows the antelope playing with the herecine tree found on the banks of the Euphrates River. Its antlers become entwined in the tree's long branches, and in frustration the antelope bellows loudly, attracting the attention of a hunter who then kills it. Thought to be symbolic of men becoming entwined with pleasures of the flesh, the moral lesson of the portrayal is to avoid becoming ensnared with sins lest one be slain by the devil. The animal's two horns are thought to represent the virtues of abstinence and obedience. Similarly, a tenth-century marble relief showing the antelope being attacked by a lion is thought to represent the human soul fighting the devil.

The antelope also holds a position of importance in Native American cultures. The antelope dance was an important ritual for many North American natives. While performing this dance, the participants moved softly, heads held erect, watching warily for enemies, as antelope do in the wild. The Hopi had an annual Snake-Antelope ceremony in which two snake maidens are greeted by two antelope youths, a symbolic marriage between the conscious and the unconscious. The antelope is thought to awaken all life energies and was often used as a symbol of fertility. Antelopes were also totem animals of the Comanche.

The Kiowa, a Plains nation from the southwestern United States, told the following story of the origin of the antelope ceremony. One day a young boy was in his grandmother's tipi when he lost her wooden spoon. She punished him, and he threw himself against the wall of the tipi, crying until he fell asleep. In his sleep he had a wonderful vision of a power that would allow him to find plentiful game in times of starvation. Many years later when the Kiowa suffered a famine, the boy called the people together and told them of his vision. They laughed at him, but the boy blew on his eagle-bone whistle and antelope fur showered down on them. Taking the incident as a spiritual sign, the people followed the young man's instructions and formed a circle on the prairie, planting arrows and singing. Horsemen galloped about, rousing game and herding it toward the circle of people until the antelopes ran into the circle. The people closed the circle so that they could hold hands, and the antelope dropped to the ground exhausted. The people then easily killed them and were able to satisfy their hunger. Whenever the people were in great need, they performed the ceremony again, and the antelopes came to them.

COMMON NAME: Armadillo, Nine-banded

SCIENTIFIC NAME: *Dasypus novemcinctus*

DESCRIPTION: Not one of God's most beautiful creatures, armadillos are rarely confused with any other animal. The head and body are 15 to 17 inches long, and the tail is about 14 inches. A hard, bony shell covers the central part of the body, the tail, and the top of the head. The snout is long and blunt, and the ears are surprisingly large.

HABITAT AND RANGE: Although it was once seen only in the extreme southeastern United States, Mexico, and South America, the armadillo is now extending its range and can be found as far north as Georgia. It prefers open, rocky areas where it can dig easily.

The strange little armadillo carries its armor on its back. When facing danger, the armadillo sometimes curls into a hard ball, but just as often it quickly burrows into the ground. Females give birth to four identical babies, always the same sex.

The animal's common name is a Spanish word meaning "little armored one," probably because of the bony plates that cover the animal so that it resembles a small medieval warrior. The plates are attached to flexible bands of skin, a system that allows the armadillo to turn and bend. An article from *Southern Living* magazine refers in fun to the armadillo as looking like "possum on the half-shell."

The armadillo's genus name *Dasypodidae* is from the Greek meaning "hairy footed ones," referring to the animal's head and toes, which bear long, scraggly hairs. Along with sloths and anteaters, armadillos are put in the order *Edentat,* from the Latin for "toothless ones." This term is a misnomer for armadillos, however, since they do have teeth. The teeth are peg-shaped and never stop growing, though they are continuously ground down by constant chewing.

The armadillo holds special fascination and honor in several South American cultures. One South American Indian tribe has even adopted the armadillo name for its own. People of the tribe believe that their shamans and medicine men take the shape of the armadillo to communicate with the Divine. Other South American tribes believe that the armadillo represents women and that men are represented by the ostrich. At the Festival of the Dead, women eat armadillo meat.

A myth from the Gran Chaco Indians of South America says that when the Creator made the first woman, the woman fell from the sky and slipped underneath the ground. An armadillo from the sky came and helped men unearth her. Armadillo then returned to the sky, and its eyes can now be seen as the two bright stars under Orion. Mayan Indians believed that the black vulture never dies, but instead turns into an armadillo.

According to Texas folklore there is only one surefire way to make an armadillo leave its hole: Reach down in there, rub its stomach to calm it down, then jerk it out.

NINE-BANDED ARMADILLO

COMMON NAME: Badger

SCIENTIFIC NAME: *Taxidea taxus*

DESCRIPTION: Badgers have short legs and wide, flattened bodies that measure 18 to 33 inches long. The tail is 4 to 6 inches in length. The gray fur is thick and shaggy, with a prominent white stripe that goes down the center of the back from the tip of the nose toward the tail. The front claws are long and sharp.

HABITAT AND RANGE: Lives in open parkland, prairies, farmlands, or forests throughout the western United States, east to the Great Lakes, south to Mexico, and north to southwest Canada. Due to the number of badgers found there in the past, Wisconsin is known as the badger state. Badgers were stamped on fifty-cent pieces issued in 1936 for the Wisconsin territorial centennial.

The name badger is a relatively new name, having been introduced in the 1500s in reference to the animal's "badge," the prominent white stripe on the center of its body. Before the sixteenth century, this animal was called *brock*, a Celtic word meaning "gray," or *bauson*, a French word meaning "fat person." The German name for badger is *dachs,* and the short-legged dogs bred to hunt these animals became known as *dachshunds,* or badger hounds.

Though badgers may look fat, they are usually very muscular. As a result, they are powerful diggers and fierce fighters. Many cultures believed the badger held important medicinal powers, a conclusion made because its excellent digging skills perhaps had given it exceptional knowledge of underground medicinal roots. For instance, Ogala Sioux attribute the same curing properties associated with the bear to the badger. Because the badger is smaller than the bear, its curative powers were used with children. Some cultures consider the badger's medicine stronger than that of the bear, as it digs deeper and more extensively into the ground.

A Native American story about the Great Flood says that the earth is really a large tortoise shell covered with dirt. White-faced people from long ago dug deep into the earth with sticks to catch badgers. One day they dug too deeply and pierced the shell. The tortoise sank and water covered the earth

A badger tooth is a talisman for good luck at card playing. The tenacity of the badger has led it to represent a "no flight, no retreat" philosophy. The expression "to badger" someone (to annoy or irritate them) does not refer to the animal's disposition, however. It derives from the cruel sport of badger baiting, in which hunting dogs are allowed to harass a badger.

One superstition suggests that the number of holes in its tail indicates how old a badger is. A natural history book written in 1867 suggested that the hairs from a badger's fur make excellent paintbrushes and the hindquarters, properly salted and cured, make good hams. Colonial Americans used badger oil to "cure" thinning hair and baldness and put it into supposedly medicinal concoctions sold for such diverse ailments as coughs, rheumatism, and sprained ankles.

In China the badger represents *Ti* in the eastern quadrant, the spring season. In Japan it is known as *tanuki* and is considered a man-eater with supernatural powers. It is a symbol of deceit and witchcraft.

BADGER

COMMON NAME: Bat, Little Brown

SCIENTIFIC NAME: *Myotis lucifugus*

DESCRIPTION: Bats are very difficult to identify to particular species, especially in flight. Bat-detectors, devices that change the ultrasonic sounds of bats to auditory wavelengths detectable by humans, are becoming more commonly used in the identification of bats. The little brown bat is the most abundant species of bats in North America. The fur is brown above and a lighter buff color below. The ears are moderately large.

HABITAT AND RANGE: The little brown bat hangs in hollow trees, caves, or abandoned buildings. It is found throughout most of the eastern United States south to central Georgia. Although often found in populated areas, these small bats seem to prefer wooded areas near water. Bat nurseries are found in caves and buildings.

In the wild, it is best to avoid coming into contact with bats, not because of their assumed association with evil, but because, like other mammals, bats are capable of transmitting diseases such as rabies.

Because of their strange shape and nocturnal habits, bats have long been considered harbingers of evil and destruction. In some cultures, however, just the opposite is true; bats are welcomed and even revered.

Bats belong to the order *Chiroptera,* from the Greek words *heir,* meaning "hand," and *pteron,* meaning "wing." The wings of bats are actually composed of long, narrow, and very strong finger bones spanned by a thin layer of leathery skin.

The genus name *Myotis* is from the Greek word *mus,* meaning "mouse," and *otis,* meaning "ear." In France bats are known as *chauve-souris,* or "bald mouse," because with their wings folded, they closely resemble mice. The Germans call them *fledermaus,* or "flutter mouse," and the Aztecs call them *quimichpapalotl,* or "butterfly mouse." The

modern English word, "bat," comes from the Middle English word, *bakke,* which means "to flutter."

Bats flying close to the ground are thought to signify an approaching storm. This superstition may hold some truth, as bats' ears are sensitive to changes in air pressure. As a storm approaches, the air pressure naturally changes, and bats fly lower to the ground to avoid these variances.

Other superstitions are less grounded in fact. Bats flying indoors were thought to be predictors of rain. A bat hanging in a tree was thought to drive away locusts. An English author wrote in 1816 that when a bat is observed to rise and then fall again, it is the witches' hour, when evil ones have power over every human being.

In Finland and Babylonia people believed

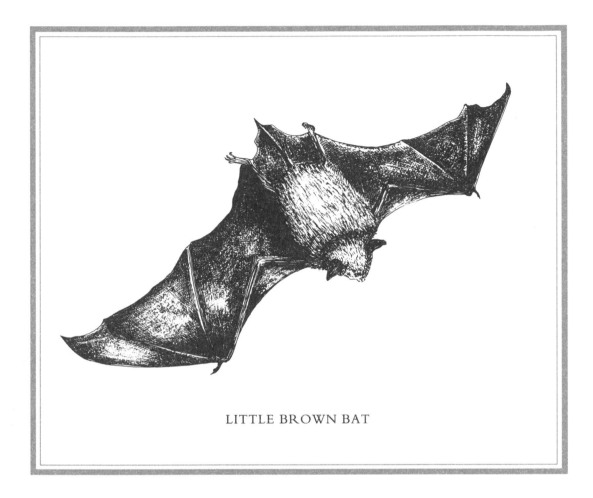

LITTLE BROWN BAT

that bats are souls of the dead. A bat flying around the outside of a house three times was thought to be a sign of immediate death, and if it flew into the house, many disasters were sure to follow. To dream of bats meant that danger is in one's future.

In eastern Europe it was believed that vampires could change into bats, a superstition supported by the existence of the actual vampire bat, which exists solely on blood. The vampire bat has an anticoagulant in its saliva so that its bite bleeds for hours. These small animals lick, rather than suck, the blood that flows from the wound.

In Finland it was thought that the soul often takes the shape of a bat while the body of the person sleeps. If approached by a bat, one was to accept it as the soul of a friend or family member. Germans believed that the heart of a bat would guard you against evil spirits.

In most Oriental countries this small mammal is symbolic of luck and light. In Japan the bat is known as *komori* and is a symbol of happiness and prosperity. The bat, peach, chrysanthemum, and endless knot together form a very common Chinese symbol that means, "May good fortune and a long life be everlasting." Five bats represent five blessings: peace, love of virtue, natural death, old age, and riches.

A Cherokee tale tells how the bat came into being. The animals challenged the birds to a game of ball. The game was about to begin when two tiny four-footed creatures came to the captain of the bird team and asked that they be allowed to play with the birds. The birds asked why they didn't play on the animal team, and the creatures replied that they had been turned away since they were so small. The bird captain felt sorry for them and agreed to let them play for the birds, offering to make wings for them.

Using a groundhog skin that had covered a ceremonial drum and tiny cane splints, the birds fashioned wings and attached them to the small animals. Thus the bat was created, and the birds won the ball game.

Bat mythology is widespread, being a part of nearly every culture with experience of its existence. In Bohemia it was believed that if one carried the right eye of a bat, it would make one invisible. A superstition from the Middle Ages suggests that if a bat became entangled in a woman's hair, the only way to remove it is to have a man cut off all the woman's hair. Another European superstition suggests that if you tie the heart of a bat to your sleeve, you will be dealt good cards, and yet another claims that burning incense over a bat buried at a crossroads is a powerful love potion.

A young woman who had little luck in attracting the man of her choice would sometimes slip a few drops of bat blood into the beer her beloved was drinking. This would supposedly kindle great desire within him and cause him to come to her.

COMMON NAME: Bear, Black

SCIENTIFIC NAME: *Ursus americanus*

DESCRIPTION: Although the common name indicates that this large mammal is all black, its fur color ranges from cinnamon to brown to black. In the Eastern United States, black is the most common color. In the West, brown or cinnamon with a white patch on the chest is common.

The black bear has a long, brown snout with a straight profile from forehead to snout. Unlike the grizzly bear, it does not have a hump on the shoulders. Head and body length is 5 to 6 feet, and the bear stands 2 1/2 to 3 feet tall at the shoulder. A mature female weighs approximately 300 pounds.

RANGE AND HABITAT: Black bears are found in forested, mountainous, and swampy areas throughout the eastern United States and in mountainous areas of the West. Other bears found in the United States include the grizzly, *Ursus arctos horribilis,* and the polar bear, *Ursus maritimus.*

Bears have always played important roles in the myths, stories, and legends of cultures throughout the world. In fact, the world's first "religious" experiences may have involved bears. For instance, it is known that Neanderthals of 100,000 years ago placed skulls of the giant cave bear in a shrinelike manner near their dwellings. This behavior indicates an awe or reverence for the animal that may have been part of one of humankind's first formal religious ceremonies.

Most of the Native American people who came into contact with bears held tremendous respect and reverence for them. Many Native Americans believed that bears held supernatural powers. The Apache believed bears to be so powerful that it was taboo to touch a bear, dead or alive.

BLACK BEAR

Native Americans who depended on the bear for food or used its fat for cooking killed the bears with great ritual and ceremony, apologizing to the bear for the indignity.

In the Native American tradition, bears are revered as an important healing animal, particularly by the Sioux. After the Sioux killed a bear, they would ceremoniously lay out the head and hide, placing the bones with particular care so the animal would not be crippled in the afterlife. The shamans of many North American people dressed as bears, believing that in this garb they would take on the supernatural healing powers of these animals.

Worship of the bear was based on the natural cycles of the bear: Hibernation represented death and emergence in spring represented rebirth. The bear cycle is similar to the cycle of death and resurrection that is an integral part of most religions.

Ceremonies involving bears fall into several distinct categories including (1) protection from bears, (2) protection by the bear's spirit, (3) healing, (4) fertility, and (5) initiation. Native American bear myths usually involve the bear mother or the bear sons. Bear mother stories often involve a she-bear spirit who found she could take human form. After going into the world as a human and marrying a man, the she-bear soon tires of people and returns to the spirit world, leaving behind her mourning husband.

Bear son stories involve half-bear/half-human brothers who go to live among the Native American peoples. They show the people how to set snares and sing ritual songs and how to show respect for the bear, thus insuring their good fortune.

The following tale is told by the Ostyak people, native to western Siberia. In the beginning, all bears lived in heaven. One day a father bear went on a hunt, and in his absence his young son mistakenly tore a hole through heaven with his sharp little paw. Peeking through the hole, the young bear saw people below and he wished to visit them. When his father returned, the bear-child pleaded with him to be allowed to visit below. The father bear eventually agreed, saying, "You can go, but you must leave the good people alone and punish the evil ones. And to all, you must teach about the great bear ceremony, the singing and the rituals." The young bear came to earth, and since that day it has served as a messenger between the world of humans and the world of the spirits.

The bear also played an important part in European literature. According to the famed Arthurian legends, Britain's King Arthur chose the bear, a symbol of power, magic, and courage, as his own emblem. Two other mythical figures, Beowulf and Odysseus, were both closely associated with the bear. The name Beowulf is an Old English form of words modern English would translate as "bee-wolf," which would mean "honey eater," or bear.

Greek myths about the bear are reminiscent of the Native American tales that involve the bear mother and/or her bear sons. In the Greek myths Callisto is the bear goddess who mated with Zeus and had Arcas. Both are now immortalized as constellations: Callisto as Ursa major, Arcas as Ursa minor.

In the Judeo-Christian tradition, the bear represents God's vengeance on the faithless. In the Old Testament's Book of Hosea it is written, "I am the Lord your God . . . they forgot me. So I will be to them like a lion, I will fall upon them like a bear robbed of her cubs." The powerful nature of the bear's influence on religion and literature is also reflected in a number of folk names for bears, which as a group indicate the combination of fear and affection in which the bear is held. Black beast, chief's son, dweller in the wilds, grandfather on the hill, little mother of honey, old man with the fur garment, and uncle of the woods are just some of these names.

Bear legend, lore, and superstition has also worked its way into our phrases and expressions. Some primitive cultures believed that mother bears actually give their tiny babies (cubs weigh $1/625$ of their mother's weight) their shape and form by licking them, thus the origin of the phrase, "licked into shape." The old saying, "like a bear sucking his paws," refers to someone who is working very hard. This phrase originated with the belief that a bear without food would suck its paws to stay alive. To "take the bear by the tooth" means to put oneself in great danger. To describe a person in a foul mood, you might use another folk saying, "He's like a bear with a sore paw."

Along with these phrases are other aphorisms like "He must have iron nails that would scratch a bear"; "The old bear falls into the old trap"; "Don't sell the skin before you catch the bear," similar to the better known saying, "Don't count your chickens before they hatch."

American folks from the Ozarks region believed that "A bad winter is betide, If hair grows thick on the bear's hide," and in some cultures it was the bear, not the groundhog, who predicted if winter would vanish on February 2 or continue another six weeks. The bear's impact, then, on folklore and superstition is emphatically obvious.

Its impact on medical science, even if without true foundation, was also great. During the sixteenth century, bear grease was thought to be powerful medicine, and it was used as a cure for baldness and to ease strained muscles. A bear's tooth was given to infants to suck on to give them strong teeth. Native North Americans believed that if you chewed on a bear's paw, you would survive a winter's sleep without needing food; if you slept on a bear skin, a backache could be cured.

The Oglala Sioux Indians consider the bear as chief of all animals in regard to herbal medicines because the fierce bear pays attention to herbs no other animal notices. The bear represents knowledge and the exploitation of underground earth forces, ie., roots and herbs. Several Asian cultures believe that certain bear body parts are powerful aphrodisiacs. Today bears in the United States are tracked and killed for these parts, which are shipped to Asia for enormous profits. This practice is threatening the natural bear populations. Asian peoples also considered the bear's paw magical and cooked it in stews to be used as a general health tonic. The testicles were thought to cure epilepsy.

An oft-told European legend tells why the bear has a short tail. Bear once had a long, bushy tail like many other animals and often bragged about its beauty, particularly to Fox, who also had a large, bushy tail. One day Fox got tired of this constant boasting from Bear and told Bear that if his tail was so long and beautiful, perhaps he could use it to fish with. Bear agreed immediately and went out onto the frozen lake. He broke a small hole in the ice and put his tail down into the water. The fish soon began nibbling, but when Bear tried to pull his tail out of the water, he found it was frozen fast in the ice and wouldn't move. In his struggles to loosen it, Bear broke off his tail. That is why today he only has a small stump of a tail, and he has never bragged about it again.

COMMON NAME: Bear, Polar

SCIENTIFIC NAME: *Ursus maritimus*

DESCRIPTION: Polar bear have massive shoulders, webbed feet, and thick, oily white fur. Their head and body length is 6 ½ to 8 feet long.

HABITAT AND RANGE: These bears are found on arctic ice floes in northern Alaska and Canada.

Polar bears figured prominently in the culture and religion of the northern tribes. When an Inuit killed a polar bear, the bear's skull was placed in the communal house, and hunters placed ceremonial gifts near it. The hunter would then feed the entire community—for four days if he had killed a male bear, for five days if a female.

Many Inuits wore a bear tooth as an amulet so they would absorb the power of the bear. It was told in Inuit legend that if a shaman desired a polar bear as his spirit animal, he would have to travel to the edge of the ice floe and call to the bears. If the bear did not kill him at once, it would sometimes agree to be the man's *tornaq*, or spirit animal. A shaman thus chosen by a polar bear was thought to be powerful enough to travel deep into the sea or high to the moon.

In the north, Nanook was a legendary great white bear.

POLAR BEAR

COMMON NAME: Bear, Grizzly

SCIENTIFIC NAME: *Ursus horribilis*

DESCRIPTION: Grizzlies stand 6 to 7 feet tall and have fur that ranges in color from yellow to dark brown. Silver tips on the fur give it a characteristic "grizzled" look. The grizzly also has a hump on its shoulder.

HABITAT AND RANGE: Grizzlies are found in mountainous forests and tundra areas from the Rocky Mountain states north into Canada and Alaska.

Seen as a heraldic figure of the city of Bern, Switzerland, as a symbol of Russia, and as the emblem of the state of California, the grizzly bear has been feared and revered throughout its history.

Trained grizzlies are often used successfully in circus acts, but they are still powerful, undomesticated animals. Grizzly Adams, a nineteenth-century American showman who lived with his trained bears for many years, was killed by one of his own bears.

The Kutenai Indians believed they were helpless against the grizzly without magic. They also believed a shaman could tap into the bear's destructive force and use it against their enemies.

The Kutenai closely associated the grizzly with the tobacco plant and considered it the plant's protector. Every year the grizzly would appear to a man of the tribe in a dream, and that individual would be the "tobacco chief" and would know the place and time to sow the seed.

The grizzly was thought to be an important healer to the Blackfoot people as well. Blackfoot shamans dressed themselves in grizzly skins to magnify the power of the medicine pipe. It was also believed by some Native American tribes that the grizzly exhaled different colors of dust—red, yellow, and blue—while it was performing healing rites.

GRIZZLY BEAR

COMMON NAME: Beaver

SCIENTIFIC NAME: *Castor canadensis*

DESCRIPTION: One of the most outstanding characteristics of the beaver is its broad, flat tail. An equally characteristic feature is the pair of large, prominent front teeth, which are orangish in color. This large rodent has blackish-brown fur and measures 3 to 4 feet in length, including the tail.

HABITAT AND RANGE: Beavers live in wetland habitats throughout the United States with the exception of Florida, California, and Nevada, where they are a bit less common. Beavers build dams and lodges from trees, sticks, and mud. As nocturnal animals, they spend much of their time during the day in the lodge, emerging in the evening to hunt and build.

The name beaver is from an old word *bhru,* which means "brown" and refers to the animal's fur. Because of the beaver's astounding ability to build dams, sometimes replacing an entire dam overnight, this remarkable mammal has come to symbolize industriousness and perseverance. Beavers also connote gentleness and wisdom in some cultures.

An old legend recorded by the Roman statesman, Pliny, says that great medicinal powers can be found in the genitals of the male beaver. According to the story a cornered beaver will bite off his own genitals and throw them to the hunter. In Christian symbolism the legend was used to represent those people who toss their souls to the devil. In art the beaver has often appeared in the act of self-mutilation, representing self-sacrifice.

In Native American legend beavers and porcupines are close companions and often play tricks on one another. Many tales from several cultures tell of beaver-husband or beaver-wife in animal marriages.

A Cheyenne legend tells that the earth rests on a single large beam. In the north country there is a beaver who is white as snow and who is father to all the animals. When the beaver is angry or in a bad mood, he gnaws at the beam. One day, the legend goes, the beaver will gnaw all the way through it, and the people and animals will fall into nothingness. Beavers were so revered among one group of the Cheyenne that they refused to eat beaver meat or to touch the skin. They would become ill, they believed, if they did touch it.

Cherokee children participated in a tradition that reflected their respect for the beaver. When a Cherokee child's first tooth fell out, the youngster took it in his or her hand and ran around the outside of his or her house four times saying, "*Da, yi, skinta,*" which means, "Beaver, put a new tooth into my jaw." Upon

BEAVER

completion of the running, the child threw the tooth onto the roof of the house. This ritual was believed to make the new tooth come in straight and strong. The beaver was invoked because of its outstanding ability to gnaw through even the hardest woods.

The emblem of the state of Oregon, the beaver is often used also as a symbol of Canada. It was placed on the original coat of arms of the city of Montreal. The first Canadian postage stamp, issued in 1851, was a "three-penny beaver."

COMMON NAME: Bison

SCIENTIFIC NAME: *Bison bison*

DESCRIPTION: Bison are very large, hooved animals with dark brown shaggy fur and curved horns. From nose to the tip of the tail measures 6 ¹/₂ to 12 feet. They are 5 to 6 feet tall at the shoulder. The longest hair is found on the head and front legs. Horns come out from the side of the head.

HABITAT AND RANGE: At one time bison roamed North America in huge herds as far east as Georgia. Today they have been reintroduced to the wild and are found mainly in prairies and open woodlands. Approximately twenty towns in the United States and several in Canada are named Buffalo.

Bison, or buffaloes as they are commonly called, formed an important part of the lives of the Plains Indians. Because these animals were so essential to the daily lives of the people, they became a central element in the religious practices. Many rituals and ceremonies involved the buffalo.

Native Americans of the Plains and southwestern and central woodlands often told tales of the buffalo. The Hidatsa of North Dakota offered food and presents to the buffalo when they needed rain, and they would sometimes dip the buffalo tail into water and shake it on the earth to bring rain.

Tribes dependent on the buffalo for food, clothing, and other uses often performed a buffalo dance for luck in the hunt. The dancers' bodies were painted, and each dancer wore a large horned headdress and sometimes a buffalo tail.

Buffalo tales are common in Native American folklore and include stories of buffalo living beneath the earth and being visited by humans. Some of the encounters resulted in buffalo–human marriages. An important

tale from the Northern Plains Indians tells of a young woman who made a pact with the buffalo to save her tribe. The tribe had created a buffalo fall, an embankment over which the buffaloes were herded and then easily killed as they fell. The big animals kept swerving to miss the fall, however, and the people were near starvation. The young woman saw a herd close by and called out to the buffaloes, "If you will jump, I will marry one of you." The herd stampeded toward the fall, and many animals were killed. One large bull separated himself from the stampede and ran to the young woman. Taking her by the arm, he carried her with him, insisting that she keep her promise.

The young woman's father soon missed her and set out to find her. He traveled only a short distance before he saw her with a small herd of buffalo. The animals sensed his presence and turned on him, trampling him until there was nothing left.

The young woman was so distraught that her buffalo-husband took pity on her and told her that if she could bring her father back to

BISON

life she could return with him to their people. The young woman found a small piece of her father's backbone and to this she sang a song of love until her father was restored. Together they returned joyfully to their people with new respect and admiration for the buffaloes.

During the mid-seventeenth century, the Cheyenne moved out of the woodlands and onto the Great Plains. In doing so they abandoned agriculture in favor of hunting. Life on the plains was made possible by the gifts of the buffalo. Its meat, bones, hide—all were used. The Summer Sun Dance, greatest of all Cheyenne ceremonies, was intended to keep the buffalo alive so that all the people might live.

Joseph Epes Brown reports in his book, *Animals of the Soul*, that Black Elk, an Oglala Sioux, wrote, "The bison is the chief of all animals, and represents the earth, the totality of all that is. It is the feminine, creating earth principle which gives rise to all living forms." Black Elk further describes the act of hunting for animals as being (not representing) life's quest for ultimate truth.

The Oglala Sioux believed that the care shown by bison for its young was highly symbolic. When a buffalo cow drops a calf in winter, she sprays it with a red filmy substance that comes from her nose and seems to help retain the calf's body heat. This instinctive buffalo behavior was reproduced by the medicine man in the rites "preparing for Woman-hood." The matriarchal role of the bison cow as a leader in the herd was seen as a model for women in the Oglala culture.

The buffalo was sometimes seen as a weather predictor. It was believed that a cold winter was coming if the buffalo's coat was very thick. Another superstition suggested that "when buffalo band together, the storm god is herding them."

The word "buff," meaning "enthusiast," dates back to the 1830s when volunteer firemen made a big show of dressing in buffalo jackets or hides.

COMMON NAME: Boar, Wild

SCIENTIFIC NAME: *Sus scrofa*

DESCRIPTION: This ancestor to the domesticated pig, originally from Europe and northern Africa, was introduced to the United States. It looks very much like the domesticated pig but is slightly larger and has coarse, thick, dark hair.

HABITAT AND RANGE: Wild, or feral, populations are found in the Appalachian regions of the southeast, and in California.

SIMILAR SPECIES: The collared peccary, or *Dicotyles tajacu,* found in southern Arizona, southern Texas, and extreme southern New Mexico.

Boars are diverse in their symbolism. In Japan the white boar represented the moon and was a symbol of courage. The Celts held it in great esteem and considered it fitting food for gods and heroes. Boars were hunted and consequently slain with great ceremony. Eating boar meat was thought to bring health and happiness. In Ireland, boars were considered magical and capable of prophesy. Druids, who were solitary forest dwellers, often called themselves boars.

The wild boar played a big part in European mythology. Perhaps the most often-told tale is of Oeneus, king of Calydon, who one year forgot to offer Artemis her customary sacrifices. In anger Artemis sent a huge boar to ravage his land. The king called upon his subjects for aid in destroying the beast, and many Greek heroes responded to his call. Among them was a beautiful Arcadian girl named Atalanta. Her presence disturbed the men. Some were jealous of her skill and powers, but others fell in love with her, including Meleager, Oeneus's son.

During the hunt, the boar was killed, but, tragically, so were two of Meleager's brothers, Meleager himself, and finally Atalanta. The sad story of the Calydonian Boar Hunt was a

WILD BOAR

favorite tale of the writers and storytellers of the ancient world.

In Scandinavian folklore the boar was shown with golden bristles, pulling the chariot of the sun across the sky. The boar became a symbol of might and strength and was depicted on the helmets of Scandinavian warriors. Thought to have the power to destroy demons, the boar was sacred to Frey and Feyja, two Scandinavian deities.

The Greeks believed that keeping or herding swine was a reputable, even enviable, position. The eating of boar was part of many rituals and ceremonies. Swine continued to play an important role in religion. Venus, goddess of fertility and love, rode a wild boar.

During the reign of Henry III, the wild boar, along with the lion and the leopard, were the animals found on the English coat of arms. King Arthur was often favorably compared to the fierce and powerful boar and is often shown with a boar's head on his shield.

In contrast to this, Egyptians considered boars evil, and Jews believe it to be the enemy of Israel and the most unclean of all animals. Swine have long been considered symbols of voracity, due to their seemingly insatiable appetites. The boar was thought particularly disgusting because it ate everything, including human flesh. Swine also became symbolic of lechery, and in medieval sculpture, the pig playing bagpipes was thought to represent lust. To dream of a boar meant bad luck in association with lust. For many centuries, pigs were arrested, tried, and condemned to death. The last record of these "pig" trials was in Yugoslavia in 1864.

According to superstition, if you met a sow in the road, you would have bad luck before you reached home, unless she happened to have her litter with her, and then you could expect good fortune. If a sow should cross in front of a wedding party, it is thought to be very unlucky, as was indicated in this quote from the *Newcastle Weekly Chronicle* in 1899: "It is unlucky to meet a pig when on the way to a wedding, a funeral, or a christening." If sailors meet a sow on the way to their ship, they turn back and postpone sailing.

In the Andaman Islands, pigs were associated with legends of female magic. The killing and preparation of pigs was done with much ceremony, and their skulls were often preserved with intricate basketry.

The smallest pig in a litter is sometimes called a "Tantony pig," referring to the patron saint of swineherds, St. Anthony.

In Hindu mythology, great floods occur every 311,040,000,000,000 years (Joseph Campbell, *The Way of Animal Powers*). During the time of the floods, the god Vishnu assumes the form of a giant boar and dives into the cosmic sea to bring back the goddess Earth.

COMMON NAME: Bobcat

SCIENTIFIC NAME: *Felis rufa*

DESCRIPTION: Total length is 2 to 3 ½ feet, including a 5-inch tail. This wildcat can weigh just over fifty pounds. The fur is thick and soft and is yellowish brown with dark brown spots. Tail has dark bands on upper side only.

HABITAT AND RANGE: The bobcat is the most common feline species in North America and is found over much of the United States, with the exception of the Midwest. Its range extends from southern Canada to southern Mexico. It is quite adaptable to a number of different habitats, including open woodland, chaparral, and swamp, and shows a moderate tolerance to the presence of humans.

The Pawnee story of creation says that Tirawa, the One Above, made the heavens and to the east was man and to the west was woman. To the east was creation planned, and to the west was creation fulfilled. Tirawa gave the evening star four beasts to

protect her, black bear, mountain lion, wolf, and bobcat. In the heavens, these were black star, yellow star, white star, and red star.

A Blackfoot legend tells the tale of why the bobcat has a short tail. An old man traveling across the Plains came to a prairie dog

BOBCAT

town. These little animals were playing an unusual game as they sat around their fire. One of them would jump into the fire, and the others would bury it with dirt and ashes. It would stay covered until it couldn't stand the heat any longer, and then it would shout, "It's hot! Let me out!" The other prairie dogs would pull the buried one out of the ashes, and another would take its turn.

The old man asked if he could play, too, and the prairie dogs looked at him suspiciously but allowed him to play. They all played for quite a while until the old man said, "Let me bury several of you at once," and the prairie dogs agreed. When the little animals began to cry out, "It's hot!" the old man just laughed, for all along he had planned on having cooked prairie dog for dinner.

When he had eaten his fill, he lay down to sleep by the fire. He was so satiated that when Bobcat crept up close to the old man, he didn't even wake up. Bobcat ate his fill of cooked prairie dogs and then went to a nearby rock to lick his paws and clean his face. The old man woke up and became very angry when he saws that Bobcat had eaten the rest of his dinner. He grabbed Bobcat by his long tail and swung him around and around until the tail broke off and Bobcat landed on its face. That's why today the bobcat's face looks as if it has been pushed in and its tail is such a tiny stump.

The Cherokee tell a similar tale. A hare enticed some turkeys to come close to a wild cat that was pretending to be asleep. As the turkeys danced around the cat, the hare jumped up and ate his fill.

The Shawnee tell why the bobcat has spots: Bobcat was chasing Rabbit and had almost caught him when Rabbit jumped into a hollow tree. Rabbit called out to Bobcat, "I'll stay in here forever; you'll never eat me!" Bobcat responded, "You'll have to come out; you'll get hungry." Rabbit knew Bobcat was right, so he called out again, saying, "Why don't you make a big fire so you can roast me as soon as I run out?"

Bobcat thought this was a good idea and built a roaring fire. As soon as the fire was hot enough, Rabbit jumped out of the tree, right into the center of the fire, scattering hot coals all over Bobcat's coat. Even though Bobcat jumped into the river and didn't catch fire, his fur was singed dark brown in every place a coal landed, and you can see those spots on his coat even today.

The species name, *rufus,* means "red" or "ruddy" and refers to the reddish tinge on the bobcat's coat.

COMMON NAME: Caribou

SCIENTIFIC NAME: *Rangifer tarandus*

DESCRIPTION: Very large deerlike animals with huge antlers, caribou stand nearly 4 feet tall at the shoulder and weigh almost 600 pounds. They have shaggy, brownish black fur with white neck, underparts, and rump. The antlers, which appear on both sexes, are huge on the males, smaller on the females.

HABITAT AND RANGE: Caribou usually travel in herds of 200 to 100,000 and are found throughout northern North America. They migrate annually, following the same routes year after year through tundra and mountain forests.

Caribou were totem animals for the Inuit and Kutchin people, and were important in Chippewayan spiritual beliefs. Caribou are also known as reindeer, and the genus name, *Rangifer,* is from the old French word meaning "reindeer." The name caribou is from *khalibu,* a name given it by the Micmac people of Newfoundland. This name means "pawer" or "scratcher," presumably because the caribou uses its paws to scratch away snow to find lichen and moss to eat.

The Reindeer Being is revered by many northern tribes. It is thought to be the being that looks after the herds. Parts of the reindeer are often used as amulets. An Eskimo tale tells of a Chukchi Reindeer Master who diminishes the reindeer herd by closing one eye. Legend holds that when he closes the other eye, the herd will disappear completely.

The traditional story of reindeer pulling Santa's sleigh may have originated with shaman rituals in Lapland. Shamans often went into trances during which it was believed the spirit actually left the body (see fly page 122) and was carried away by a sleigh pulled by reindeer.

Another Lapp belief was that the Germanic god Otlin (also known as Odin, Wodin,

CARIBOU

and Wotan) flew through the sky on the first night of the new year. He brought presents for those who worshipped him and punishments for those who did not. This belief perhaps led to the Lapp practice of making sacrifices to the Great Reindeer deity to ensure good luck for the herd.

An Eskimo tale tells of how the people once asked their shaman to find out where the reindeer went when they left the coast. The shaman, or *angakok,* asked his helping spirit for assistance, and the spirit said that he would show him where the reindeer went but warned that if the shaman or his people ever killed one of them, or even wished to kill one,

the spirit would change him into the lowliest creature on the earth. The spirit and the shaman traveled together into the Inland Ice, and the shaman saw the reindeer—the most beautiful sight he had ever seen. When he returned, the shaman did not dare tell the people about the reindeer because he was afraid they might kill one of the animals and he would be turned into a maggot.

Ernest Thompson Seton wrote in 1911, "The caribou is a travelsome beast, always in a hurry going against the wind. When the wind is west, all travel west: when it veers, they veer."

COMMON NAME: Chipmunk, Eastern

SCIENTIFIC NAME: *Tamias striatus*

DESCRIPTION: The total body length of the eastern chipmunk is 9 to 12 inches. Almost half this length is made up of a bushy brown tail. Body coloring is reddish brown with distinctive black (or dark brown), buff, and white stripes. These stripes are also found on the head. The ears are small and erect, and the eyes are small, shiny, and dark.

HABITAT AND RANGE: The eastern chipmunk is abundant in open woodland and suburban areas, particularly along rock walls. This species is found throughout the eastern United States, north into southeastern Canada, and south to northern Florida and Louisiana.

SIMILAR SPECIES: Sixteen other species of chipmunks are found in the western United States. These are, in general, smaller and more slender than the eastern chipmunk and include the Pine Chipmunk, *Eutamias amoenus*, Colorado chipmunk, *E. quadrivittatus*, and the least chipmunk, *E. minimus*, which is widespread throughout the Rocky Mountain states and into Canada.

The name chipmunk does not come from the characteristic "chip, chip" sound of the animal itself, as is commonly thought. It may be a corruption of the Chippewa word for red squirrel, *chetamon,* or the Algonquian word, *atchitamon,* meaning "headfirst" and referring to the animal's habit of running down tree trunks in that position. The genus name *Tamias* is Greek for "one who stores," or "a hoarder." The species name *striatus* means striped.

Chipmunks figure largely in folktales and legends and are often linked with bears in these tales. In Russia, the chipmunk's name means "the bear's conscience." An Iroqois legend tells how the chipmunk received its stripes. Long ago the world was all dark, and the animals gathered to decide if it would be better to remain in darkness or to bring in light. Bear wanted darkness, but little Chipmunk argued for light. When light began to appear with the first sunrise, Chipmunk was so happy he began to sing and shout. Bear was angry that he didn't get his way and tried to grab at Chipmunk. Chipmunk managed to get away, but only after Bear's claw scratched his back. Even today you can see these long, dark marks.

A different version of this story comes from India. It suggests that the chipmunk helped the god Rama to cross the sea between India and Ceylon, and when they were safely across, Rama gently stroked the chipmunk's back, leaving the marks of his fingers.

Among the Hopi people of the American Southwest, chipmunks were considered runner kachinas, a spirit of the natural world. The runner kachinas would challenge men to

EASTERN CHIPMUNK

races during festivals. If the men won, the kachinas bestowed great gifts on them. If the men lost, they were punished. Legend holds that if a runner lost to the chipmunk, he would be beaten with a yucca whip. The chipmunk kachina is often depicted with its yucca whip as a doll or in art. Chipmunks are also included in Navajo sandpaintings, which were used in healing rituals. Chipmunk's wife is often included in the paintings. She is known as the spirit of sunset.

The Navajo believe that it is bad luck to kill chipmunks, for these little creatures are thought to lead travelers to food and water.

COMMON NAME: Coyote

SCIENTIFIC NAME: *Canis latrans*

DESCRIPTION: This member of the dog family has grey fur, sometimes tinged with red, and a bushy tail with a dark tip. Coyotes are smaller than wolves, but larger than the red fox. They stand almost 2 feet tall at the shoulder. From nose to tail they generally measure 3 to 4 feet.

HABITAT AND RANGE: Coyotes are abundant and live in almost every area of the mainland United States except the extreme southeast. While originally only found in open prairies and grasslands, coyotes have now extended their range to include urban areas as well. Although they are often accused of preying on livestock, they most often eat small animals, such as rabbits and rodents.

The folklore surrounding the coyote is rich and extensive. From the Aztec and Mayan civilizations of Mexico to almost all Native American peoples living west of the Mississippi River, many cultures believed the coyote had magical powers.

Coyote, known as Medicine Dog, Brother, Old Man Coyote, or Little Wolf, represents diverse characteristics. Said to love poetry and characterized sometimes as a clown, the coyote is also accused of introducing death, pain, and evil to the world. The cunning nature of this animal earned it a place as the trickster in many Native American folk stories. It was also depicted as a transformer and considered a primary actor in creation stories.

Many stories tell how Coyote fashioned humans from feathers, mud, and straw. In the Chinook region it is told that Coyote was created from a fog that filled the earth after the flood. He wove various feathers together, which later became people of different tribes. In legends from the native people of Califor-

nia, other creator animals include Eagle, Wolf, and Fox, all of which create good. Coyote, however, brings death because he knew that if all people lived forever, they would run out of food.

After creating humans Coyote brought many gifts to the people. According to Zuni legend, coyote taught man to hunt; the Sioux believed he taught humans about useful plants. Indians of the Pacific Northwest tell how Coyote put salmon in the rivers and taught men how to make fish traps and salmon spears. The Seri people say that Coyote taught them to take the sweet juice out of the cactus.

When the world was first created, the buffalo had such keen eyesight that hunters could not come close without the buffalo running away. Coyote is said to have taken pity on the hunters, kicking sand in the buffaloes' eyes to make them nearsighted, a condition that remains to this day.

As a trickster, Coyote is often accompa-

COYOTE

nied by another animal such as Wolf, Wild-cat, Porcupine, Badger, or Fox. In this role, the coyote and its friends live and talk as people. These tales tell about a prehuman mythical age. Trickster Coyote is involved in escapades that result in his stealing fire or daylight, freeing trapped animals, or teaching others about various arts and crafts. The stories often take on an erotic or obscene theme in which Coyote is portrayed as a lecherous, greedy bully. These tales were meant to amuse as well as to teach a moral lesson.

A Hopi story tells that Coyote created the Milky Way when he took the lid off a sealed pot and allowed the stars to escape. Many different cultures tell that Coyote brought fire. This tale has many different variations. The following is a Plains Indians account:

Coyote watched the people and saw how happy they were during the warm summer months and how cold and miserable they were when winter came. He decided to do something to help the people. He knew of a mountaintop far away where there were three Fire Beings. Here they kept fire all to themselves, not sharing with anyone. Coyote decided to visit them and steal a bit of the fire so people could be warm during the months of snow and cold.

At the mountaintop, Coyote saw the Fire Beings standing guard over the fire as always, not allowing anyone or anything to come close. Coyote waited patiently all through the night. Early in the morning, when all the Fire Beings were asleep, he leapt to the fire and grabbed a flaming stick. He ran like the wind back to the people.

Even though Coyote ran fast, the Fire Beings, furious that someone had stolen their fire, ran after him and caught him. One Fire being reached out and touched the tip of Coyote's tail, which immediately turned white. Coyote called out and threw the fire to Squirrel, who ran away with the flame. The Fire Beings caught him, too, and touched his back so that his long tail curled up and over, as it does today. Squirrel threw the fiery stick to Chipmunk, who also ran. He, too, was finally caught by a Fire Being who scraped long fingers down Chipmunk's back, leaving three black stripes. Chipmunk threw the fire to Frog, who jumped away, but not before one of the Fire Beings had grabbed his long tail and broken it off (which is why frogs have no tail today). Frog threw the fire to Wood, who swallowed it.

The Fire Beings could not figure out how

to get fire from the wood. They finally left and went back home in defeat. But Coyote knew how to get fire from the wood. He taught the people to rub two sticks together to bring out the fire, which kept them warm from that day forward.

As a transformer, Coyote was said to have moved mountains, dried up lakes, altered the courses of rivers, and changed the path of the sun to give more light and warmth to the people. He made these changes to correct mistakes made when the earth was created.

It is also told that when the earth was first created, all the plants were in neat rows and the stars were all lined up. Coyote changed all this, throwing the stars in all directions and flinging seeds in the air, allowing them to drop and grow wherever they landed. Coyote changed animals as well. In the very beginning dogs had the power of speech, but they went around the villages spreading gossip and trouble. Coyote took speech from them so that today they can only howl and bark.

Another Hopi story tells why the coyote has yellow eyes. Long ago Skeleton Man lived close to Coyote Woman. One day Skeleton Man sang a song and his eyes flew out of his head and out of sight. In a few moments, his eyes reappeared and flew back into his head. "I have seen so much!" Skeleton Man told Coyote Woman. "I have seen much game in that canyon far to the south."

Now Coyote Woman wanted to see the game. "Teach me the song, so that my eyes can see the canyon," she called to Skeleton Man. Skeleton Man answered, "You must stand very still and face the south and do not move," and he taught her the song. Coyote Woman sang the song and her eyes flew out of her head. She could see much, but, in her excitement, she turned to the north and her eyes never came back to her.

Soon Coyote Woman could not see anything. She felt around on the ground to find her eyes, and when she found something big and round, she popped it into her head, thinking it was an eye. Then she found another one and popped that into her head and went to find her children. Unfortunately, she had put gourds into her head instead of eyes, and when her children saw her with her big yellow eyes, they were scared and ran away. That is why today the coyote has big yellow, scary eyes.

Coyotes are the subject of much symbolism and superstition. For instance, shamans who had the coyote as a guardian spirit were thought to be unusually powerful. The Comanche say that at one time their people could converse with the coyotes, the language having been taught to them by a boy raised by coyotes. It was believed that if a coyote barked directly at you or at your lodge, someone in the family would die soon.

In Mexico coyotes are closely associated with black magic, and Mexicans often carried a small coyote bone or tuft of hair to keep away witches. It is thought that if one tried to ride a horse in the tracks of a coyote, the horse will stumble and fall. Mexican hunters claim that if a coyote crosses a hunter's path, game will not be found. A widely held Mexican belief says that coyotes will repay those who help them. This Mexican proverb shows the great reverence in which this animal was held: "Next to God the coyote is the smartest person on Earth."

Because coyotes were such an integral part of life in the American West, several proverbs from that region deal with coyotes. When one said, "The coyote won't get another chicken from me," it meant that one had learned a valuable lesson. To have "heard the coyote bark" meant that one had extensive experiences.

Many people believed that a coyote could hypnotize its prey with its tail or with its eyes.

South Dakota is called the coyote state. The species name *latrans,* means "barker," or "one who barks."

COMMON NAME: Deer, White-tailed

SCIENTIFIC NAME: *Odocoileus virginianus*

DESCRIPTION: A tall, graceful animal, the white-tailed deer measures about 4 to 6 feet in length and stands 2 to 3 1/2 feet at the shoulder. Weight varies from 50 to 300 pounds. Males usually start growing antlers a few months after birth; antlers are usually absent in females. The fur is reddish brown, turning grayish brown in winter. The tail is long (6 to 11 inches) and distinctly white underneath.

HABITAT AND RANGE: White-tailed deer are found throughout the United States except in the Far West. They prefer open woodland, pastures, or farmland.

SIMILAR SPECIES: The mule deer, *Odocoileus hemionus*, is found in all western states. More intolerant of human activity than the white-tailed deer, it is most often seen in early morning or late evening. The mule deer is a medium-sized deer with yellowish brown fur, a white rump, and a black-tipped tail. The ears are large and mule-like. Preferred habitat is similar to that of the white-tailed deer.

Contrary to popular belief, the size of a deer's antlers has more to do with nutrition than age, and thus the age cannot be determined by how large the antlers are.

The genus name *Odocoileus* is from the Greek words *odous*, meaning "tooth," and *koilos*, meaning "hollow," referring to the hollow teeth of deer.

Many Native American tribes hold an ambivalent attitude toward deer and other animals with forked horns or antlers because they believe the characteristic represents a forked or double nature. The white-tailed deer was thought to be an animal helper, but the dark-tailed deer represented danger. Some Native Americans believed that the dark-tailed deer could change itself into a beautiful maiden, changing the peculiar odor of her hoof into a perfume that helped her lure young men. If a young man approached her, she would change back into a doe, and the young man would die soon afterward. If by chance he survived this encounter with the doe, the man would possess great power for the rest of his life.

A Cherokee legend tells how the deer received its antlers. In the beginning, Deer had a smooth head and was very fast. Rabbit, too, was a fast runner. One day the animals decided to have a contest to determine which of the two was faster. They laid out the race path through thickets and trees and fashioned a pair of antlers as a prize for the winner.

Rabbit asked if he could look at the path before the race, and the animals agreed. He took so much time, however, that they sent a messenger to see what he was up to. The messenger found Rabbit cutting down vines and shrubs, making himself a clearer path on which to run. The animals considered this cheating, and they awarded the antlers to

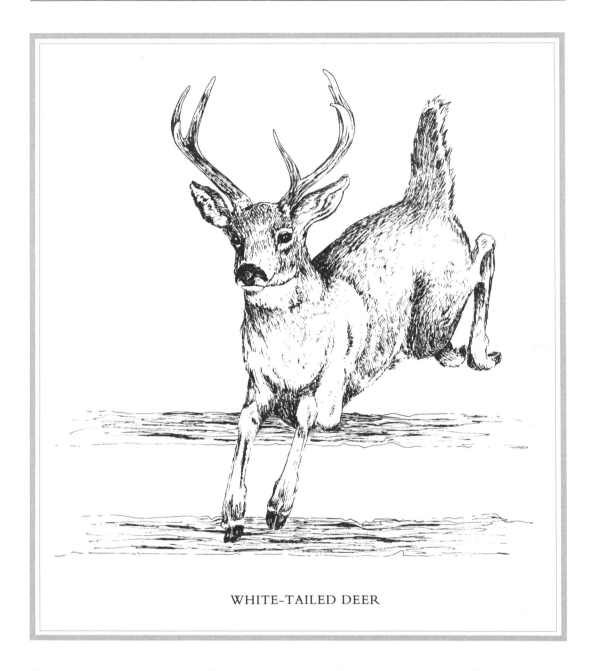

WHITE-TAILED DEER

Deer, who has worn them proudly ever since.

The deer was believed to be a rain bringer, and the deer dance, performed by many Native American tribes, was thought to bring good fortune. The Hopi deer dance was to bring rain, the California Yurok White Deer Dance was for bountiful wild crops, and the Zuni deer dance was to effect a cure.

The Yaqui Indian name for deer was Maso, and this name also applied to the Yaqui deer dance, part of the religion of the woods. During the dance, the principal players wear only a deer head with big glass eyes and horns decorated with red tassels and flowers.

When the Cherokee had to travel during harsh winter months, they rubbed their feet in warm ashes and sang a song to acquire powers from the four animals whose feet are never frostbitten—opossum, wolf, fox, and deer.

Deer antlers, ground and mixed with herbs, were thought to cure impotency. A young buck, boiled in its velvet (the soft skin on the antlers), was used to treat dropsy.

The deer is considered a universal symbol of agility, swiftness, and gentleness. Deer were sacred to the Egyptian deity, Isis, but the actual animals became extinct in that part of the world before the Christian era. Deer were also considered sacred to the Greek goddesses Artemis, Aphrodite, Athene, and Diana. In the Bible, the deer is referred to as a hart or hind. The deer was used as the emblem for Saint Henry.

When Buddha gave his first sermon at the deer park at Sarnath, he set the Wheel of the Law into action. Deer, which represent meditation, gentleness, and meekness, are often shown on either side of the Wheel.

Many hunters believed that to kill a deer on Sunday was thought to bring bad luck.

COMMON NAME: Elk

SCIENTIFIC NAME: *Cervus elaphus*

DESCRIPTION: Elk stand up to 4½ feet tall at the shoulder, and the males carry magnificent antlers. Males are larger than females, but in general these deer measure 7½ to 9½ feet long and have a short, 6- to 8-inch tail. Coloration is reddish brown with pale rump and tail. (Elk are sometimes called *wapiti*, a Native American word for "white," referring to the pale rump.)

HABITAT AND RANGE: Now confined to the Rockies, elk were at one time found throughout North America. They are seen most often in mountain meadows and forests. Some authorities believe this is the same species as the Eurasian red deer.

Elks are symbolic of stamina and strength and are said to possess warrior energy. During the Gallic Wars, Julius Caesar offered the following advice for hunting elk. He said that during the night the elk sheds its antlers, and its legs become jointless so he can sleep standing up, leaning against a tree. To capture the elk, it was necessary to dig beneath the tree so that as the elk leaned against it, the tree would fall and the elk with it.

An elk often appears as an animal character in legends and tales from the Great Basin or the Plains states. One recurring tale is of a giant elk conquered by a human hero, usually a young boy, with the help of a mouse. The Apache people say that this human hero is

ELK

called Killer-of-Enemies or Child-of-the-Water. Tales of elk husband or wife are also frequently told on the Plains.

In origin legends of Oto, it was Elk who gave people fire and taught them to build villages. The Oglala Sioux also revere the elk for its strength, speed, and courage.

Elk societies seem fascinated by the fact that the bull elk can whistle or bugle and cows are irresistibly drawn to him. Clark Wissler, in *Animals of the Soul*, says "The elk is taken as the incarnation of the power over females. The Indian believes that the elk possesses knowledge necessary to the workings of the power (conceived of nature). Thus a

mythical elk becomes the teacher of man."

Even after an elk dies and begins to decay, its teeth remain intact and will remain after everything else has crumbled to dust. The teeth are said to last longer than the life of a man, and thus the elk tooth became an emblem of a long life. Among the Plains Indians, elk teeth are highly valued as costume ornaments.

Ground elk hoof has long been used in folk medicine as a cure for vertigo. This treatment derives from the superstition that the elk itself often gets dizzy and cures itself by placing its left hind foot in its left ear.

COMMON NAME: Ferret, Black-footed

SCIENTIFIC NAME: *Mustela nigripes*

DESCRIPTION: Having a long body and short, dark legs, the black-footed ferret is only 18 to 20 inches long, including a 5-inch tail. It weighs 1 1/2 to 2 1/2 pounds. Most of the fur is a yellow-buff color. The tip of the tail, the face mask, and the feet are black.

HABITAT AND RANGE: Nearly extinct in the wild, one colony of the black-footed ferret is known to live at the base of the Absaroka mountains in Wyoming.

The ferret most often sold in pet stores is a fitch ferret, often erroneously called the black-footed ferret. The fitch has been domesticated since the fourth century B.C. Its original use was not as a pet but as a

hunter of rabbits, and it was used for this purpose by Persians, Greeks, and Romans. The true black-footed ferret is neither sold in pet stores nor kept in zoos.

The name ferret is from the Latin word

BLACK-FOOTED FERRET

fur, meaning "a thief." The Sioux gave the black-footed ferret the name *Pispiza etopta sapa,* which means "black-faced prairie dog." The Pawnee referred to it as a ground dog and thought that it had special powers.

The people of the Crow nation used the skins, stuffed with cotton and decorated with leather, feathers, and ornaments, as medicine bags. The Cheyenne and Blackfoot used ferret fur to decorate their headdresses.

Black-footed ferrets depend almost entirely on prairie dogs for food. Since the drastic reduction of prairie dog populations, the black-footed ferret has neared extinction.

To "ferret out" something means to dig deeply or uncover.

COMMON NAME: Fox, Red

SCIENTIFIC NAME: *Vulpes fulva*

DESCRIPTION: The red fox resembles a medium-sized dog, measuring 2 to 3 1/2 feet in length, including a 12- to 17-inch bushy tail with a white tip. Black is shown on the feet and the backs of the ears. Though reddish fur is most common, black or silver coloration is sometimes seen, as well as individuals with a "cross" or dark markings on the shoulder.

HABITAT AND RANGE: The red fox prefers open areas such as sparsely wooded areas, fields, and farmland and also more populated areas like golf courses and cemeteries. Red foxes are found throughout the United States and Canada except for parts of the southwestern and Rocky Mountain states.

SIMILAR SPECIES: This species is very similar to the Old World fox, *V. vulpes,* which is native to all of Europe, temperate Asia, and northern Africa. The gray fox, *Urocyon cinereoargenteus*, is also widespread in the United States and south to Mexico. Unlike other members of the dog family, the gray fox easily climbs trees. This species has coarse salt-and-pepper fur and orange markings underneath and on the back sides of the ears. The arctic fox, *Alopex lagopus,* is all white in winter and brown or grayish white in summer.

The fox figures prominently in many different cultures. In China and Japan, people believed fox spirits shared the world with humans. These spirits were powerful but not particularly friendly to humans. If you pleased the fox spirit, it would reward you richly. If you made it angry, you would be punished. In Oriental lore foxes were called "shape-shifters," meaning they could take many different forms, including human.

The fox is one of the five main animals of Chinese lore. A black fox is considered good luck, a white fox signals calamity, and three foxes mean disaster. In Japan, the fox is called *kitsune* and is a magical animal said to be able to cast spells, bewitch people, and assume human shape. All foxes are thought to be malicious except the Inari fox, messenger of the harvest god. The Japanese make sacrifices at special shrines to appease foxes.

The Greek god of wine, Dionysus (also known as Bacchus), was associated with the fox, protecting the vineyards from the "little foxes" that spoiled the grapes. The Greek slave Aesop told the following story of the fox and grapes: A hungry fox sees a delicious clump of grapes just out of its reach. It tries and tries to reach them but cannot do so and finally walks away saying they were probably sour anyway. The moral? It is easy to belittle what you cannot get.

Another fable involves the fox and a crane. The fox invites the crane to a meal and serves him soup in a flat dish, from which the crane cannot eat. The crane then invites Fox to his house and serves him soup in a long-necked

RED FOX

bottle, from which the fox cannot eat. The moral is that turnabout is fair play.

The Bible mentions raids that foxes made on ripening grapes in the vineyards of ancient Israel. In Christian lore, the fox represents the devil as deceiver.

During the Middle Ages *The Tales of Renard the Fox* were quite popular. This medieval collection of poems composed in northern France depicts Renard outsmarting Isengrim the Wolf and Nobel the Lion. Many of the tales are illustrated with foxes wearing monks' clothes. They were shown to satirize friars who wandered the countryside telling people of corruption in the organized church. Renard was often shown imbibing to excess, thus the phrase "to be foxed" means to get intoxicated. Other French sayings about the fox include:

"The tail doth often catch the fox."
"An old fox understands the trap."
"He that will get the better of a fox must rise early."
"A wise fox will never rob his neighbor's henroost."

In western cultures, the fox played a prominent role in trickster tales, often as companion to Coyote, not only in Native

American stories but also in southern black culture as well, as evidenced by Uncle Remus' Bre'r Fox. Fox is seen as wily, crafty, and cunning.

In an Eskimo tale a man comes home each night to find that his house has been put in order by a mysterious guest. One day he hides near his home and sees a fox enter his house. He goes inside and finds that the fox has turned into a beautiful woman, whom the man marries. One day he asks his wife about a musky odor in house, and the wife admits that she gives forth the odor. She takes off her skin clothing, resumes her foxskin, and quietly slips away from the house never to return. This story is one of many similar tales that represents an offended supernatural wife.

The fox was important to many Native American tribes, and among the Oglala Sioux, Fox Societies were often formed. The fox was considered persistent, yet gentle, and less aggressive than the wolf. Wolf societies dealt with warfare, but fox societies centered on camp life and hunting.

The fox was thought to have knowledge of underground things hidden from human eyes. If one dreamt of the fox or saw one in a vision, one would absorb some of the fox's power of swiftness, cleverness, and gentleness.

According to these proverbs, "a fox should not be jury at the goose's trial," and "the fox may grow gray but never good."

In Ireland they say that the fox displays three traits: a light step, a look to the front, and glance to each side of the road.

An old superstition says that the fox will rid itself of fleas by picking up a piece of sheep's wool and swimming out into the river until it is submerged except for the tip of its nose. The fleas will then jump off the fox and onto the sheep wool.

General Erwin Rommel was a World War II German commander who was nicknamed "the Desert Fox."

COMMON NAME: Gopher, Western Pocket

SCIENTIFIC NAME: *Thomomys sp.*

DESCRIPTION: There are several species of western pocket gophers and several species of eastern pocket gophers, *Geomys sp.* The eastern pocket gophers do not have the characteristic grooves down the center of their front teeth.

In general, gophers are mid-sized furry animals measuring 5 to 10 inches in length, including a 2- to 3-inch naked tail. The claws are long and sharp. The large teeth are used for digging and are clearly visible even when the animal's mouth is closed. They have outside fur-lined cheek pouches. Individual species are difficult to tell apart and are best determined by range.

HABITAT AND RANGE: Pocket gophers occur only in North and Central America and are found most frequently in areas with loose, sandy soil, such as prairies, meadows, and deserts.

The Oglala Sioux regarded gophers as negative spirit animals. If someone developed sores on their neck or under their jaw, it was believed to have been caused by gophers. They were thought to wound people by shooting at them with certain grasses.

To the Blackfoot people, gophers represented a state of distraction or a casual attitude, two traits disliked by Plains Indians, whose very survival depended on staying aware and focused.

A Cheyenne legend tells of how seven brothers and a gopher saved their sister. Seven brothers lived all alone. Not far from them lived a young girl with her grandmother. One day the grandmother made seven buffalo robes and seven pair of moccasins and gave them to the girl, whose name was Red Leaf. The grandmother sent Red Leaf to give the brothers the robes and moccasins and to ask the brothers if she could be their sister. The brothers welcomed her as their sister, and they all lived happily together until one day when the brothers were hunting and the dreaded Double-teeth bull kidnapped Red Leaf from their home. When the brothers returned from hunting, they grieved and left immediately to find their sister. They finally found her lying on the ground on the Plains, with Double-teeth bull close by.

The youngest brother had brought a gopher skin, which he took out and put on the ground. It immediately became a live gopher, who quickly dug a tunnel underground straight to Red Leaf. The younger brother followed in the tunnel, and when he came to the girl, he took her hand and led her back to his brothers. When Double-teeth bull realized Red Leaf was gone, he and the other buffaloes ran to retrieve the girl and kill her brothers. The brothers and Red Leaf had climbed a giant tree up to the sky, however, and today they are still there as seven stars. The girl is the head star, and the small one off to the side is the youngest brother, who is still standing guard.

The name gopher is from the French word *gaufre*, meaning "a honeycomb"; it refers to the underground maze the gopher digs. The genus name *Thomomys* is from the Greek words *thomos*, "a heap," and *mus*, "a mouse." These words refer to the heaps of earth found along the gopher's burrows.

WESTERN POCKET GOPHER

COMMON NAME: Groundhog

SCIENTIFIC NAME: *Marmota monax*

DESCRIPTION: Groundhogs measure 16 to 24 inches, including a 4- to 6-inch tail. They weigh four to twelve pounds at maturity. The fur is dark brown, grizzled with gray. Legs are short and dark, ears small and erect, tail dark and bushy.

HABITAT AND RANGE: Common in the eastern half of the United States south to northern Alabama. Also found in western Canada and Alaska. Their preferred habitat is open forest or meadow, roadsides, and suburban areas.

———

These small rodents are called by a variety of names, most commonly woodchuck or groundhog. Groundhogs have long been associated with Candlemas Day, February 2. According to tradition, on this date the groundhog will come above ground. If it sees its shadow in the sunshine, it is a sign that winter will linger for six more weeks. If the small animal does not see its shadow, it will venture out, indicating that there will be an early spring. In the Old World, it was the badger that was given credit for predicting the weather.

Meteorologists and naturalists have kept careful records for decades and have concluded that the weather on February 2 has little to do with the weather for the remainder of the winter months. Further, the groundhog is not a good animal indicator because it generally hibernates through February and rarely appears above ground. Nevertheless, Americans turn to Punxsutawney, Pennsylvania, every February 2 to hear the official report from the Groundhog Club, which has closely watched its groundhogs every year since 1898.

The groundhog appears in many animal . The Cherokee claim that in the old days, when animals talked and lived with people, marriages between humans and woodchucks were common. They also tell that Groundhog used to have a long, luxuriant tail, but that one day he ran into a pack of wolves who began to chase him. Groundhog was frightened, but told the wolves that he would teach them a new dance before he died. The wolves were hungry, but they wanted to learn a new dance so they agreed. Groundhog danced and danced, and the wolves began to dance, too. Finally Groundhog danced around to his hole and quickly dove under the ground to safety. The wolves were quick behind him, though, and as he disappeared, they grabbed his tail, which broke off and has been short ever since.

The Mohawks say that in the old days both animals and people lived underneath the ground until one day the fire god, Gamawagehha, noticed a tiny crack in the earth's surface and went to investigate. He crawled through this crack up into the air and light above and returned below to tell everyone of the beautiful place he had been. One by one the animals and people crawled through the crack in the surface to live above

GROUNDHOG

ground, all except the woodchuck, who was happy and content to live deep in the ground.

Among the Zuni Indians, the gopher was considered an important animal curer. In North Carolina, woodchuck soup was thought to cure whooping cough.

The groundhog, like other animals, found its way into our language. New Englanders described people who weren't very intelligent as those who couldn't tell "a woodchuck from a skunk." To feel like a "woodchuck in clover" means that a person is quite happy. A favorite tongue twister was "How much wood could a woodchuck chuck if a woodchuck could chuck wood? A woodchuck would chuck all the wood he could chuck if a woodchuck could chuck wood."

COMMON NAME: Horse, Wild

SCIENTIFIC NAME: *Equus caballus*

DESCRIPTION: Very similar to the domestic pony or horse, the wild mustang is approximately 6 1/2 to 7 1/2 feet in length, with a long 19-inch tail. The tail and mane distinguish the wild horse from burros.

HABITAT AND RANGE: Seen almost always in grassland and prairies throughout the western United States.

Horses have always been closely associated with humans and have been both useful and sacred. A principal symbol of fertility, power, fleetness, and wisdom, the wild horse was seen as a spirit of the field who runs across the tops of the grain with the wind.

The following is from a Hindu religious treatise by Brihadaranyaka Upanishad: "The head of the celestial horse is the dawn, its eye the sun, its breath the air, its open mouth a fire . . . Its back is heaven, its belly the sky . . . its feet the days and nights, its bones the stars and its flesh the clouds." The horse was a virtual creation myth unto itself.

The Navajo of Arizona tell how Johano-ai, the Sun, leaves his hogan in the east and every day rides across the skies to his hogan in the west, carrying a shining, golden disk. He has five horses, all different colors, which ate flower blossoms and drank holy waters. When Johano-ai rides his turquoise horse or his horse of white shell or pearl, the skies are blue with white clouds scuttling across. When he rides the red horse or the horse of coal, the skies are laden with storm clouds.

The introduction of the horse by the Spaniards to the Native Americans revolutionized their existence. The Indians learned quickly and easily how to handle these "magic dogs" of the white man. With the horse, the Indians could either keep up with the buffalo herds or travel to them and hunt and return to camp by nightfall. Indians regularly stole horses from the Spaniards and traded them between tribes. Soon horses became a symbol of power and importance. Each tribe created its own legend of how it first received the horse. The Nez Percé Indians were so taken by the beautiful markings on some horses that they bred these animals for their coloration and created the Appaloosa.

The Norse god, Frey, who was responsible for rain and sunshine, held the horse sacred. Greek mythology finds the horse associated with Poseidon, god of the sea. Poseidon was said to have a stable of horses with golden manes and bronze hooves underneath the sea.

The Greek hero Heracles (Hercules in Latin) was forced to perform twelve labors as punishment for killing his children while suffering from madness imposed by Hera, the wife of Zeus. The eighth of these labors involved the wild flesh-eating horses owned by Diomedes, king of Thrace. Heracles cap-

WILD HORSE

tured the horses but was pursued by Diomedes. The horses became impossible to handle and killed Abderus, a friend and companion to Heracles. Finally Heracles killed Diomedes and fed his flesh to the horses who immediately became quiet and docile.

In many cultures, white feet on a horse were thought to be significant. A fifteenth-century rhyme from a Bodleian plate says if your horse has four white feet, give him to your foe, if three, do even so, but if he has two, give him to a friend. If he has just one, keep him till the end.

In many cultures worldwide, different horses under different circumstances are believed to bring good or bad luck. In India,

Great Britain, and the United States, it is lucky to dream of horses and lucky to see one. Folk custom dictated that if a piebald horse walks by, spit three times, count to ten, and your wish will come true.

Many superstitions deal with white horses. One of these states that if you wish on the first white horse you see on New Year's Day, your wish will come true. Another states that it is unlucky for a bridal pair to drive behind two white horses. One superstition suggests that if you see a white horse, you will soon see a redheaded girl. In northern Canada a folk belief states that you will die within the year if you watch a herd of white horses go out of sight.

The white horse is rich in symbolism in Persia, Greece, Rome, Scandinavia, China, and Japan. In Iran, the chariot of Ardvisura Anahita is pulled by four white horses that represent wind, rain, cloud, and sleet. Pegasus, the white winged horse of poetry, originally carried thunder and lightning for the Greek god, Zeus.

Muslim's believe that the horse is an animal sent from God and capable of foreseeing danger and of seeing the dead. Some cultures believed that horses can see ghosts, and it was sometimes thought that horses are ghosts.

One of Aesop's fables tells of a horse and a stag. One day a stag wandered into a horse's pasture and ate all the rich, green grass. This angered the horse and he decided to punish the stag. He asked a man to help, and the man agreed to do so only if the horse would allow him to put a saddle on him and a bit in his mouth. Once the horse was saddled, the man would not release him, and the horse has been domesticated ever since.

In many cultures the horse was seen as a symbol of sexual virility. In France during medieval times, it was believed that the mistresses of priests turned into black mares at their death. The caves at Lascaux show prehistoric drawings of various animals. The drawings are divided into male/female, or yin/yang. On one side are those animals considered "female"—the ox and bison. On the other side are "male" animals, which include the stag, and particularly, the horse. According to archeologists and anthropologists, the animals most important to these paleolithic peoples were the bison and the horse. The horses pictured in these caves are "wooly ponies," much like ones found in Iceland today.

COMMON NAME: Lemming, Southern Bog

SCIENTIFIC NAME: *Synaptomys cooperi*

DESCRIPTION: A small rodent, only $4^{1}/_{2}$ to 6 inches long, including its short ($^{1}/_{2}$ to 1 inch) tail, the lemming weighs only about an ounce. The fur is brown, grizzled with gray, turning to gray on the belly. Fur-covered ears are small and almost hidden. Distinctive grooves mark the upper incisor teeth.

HABITAT AND RANGE: From Quebec west to Manitoba and Kansas and south to North Carolina, the southern bog lemming is found not in swampy areas or bogs as the name would imply but in grassy areas and meadows.

SIMILAR SPECIES: The northern bog lemming, *S. borealis*, is very similar to the southern species. It inhabits marshy areas throughout Canada. The brown lemming, *Lemmus trimucronatus* has reddish brown fur. The soles of the feet are covered in stiff hairs that aid in digging. This species lives from the Alaskan peninsula through Canada to Hudson's Bay and south to the Rockies.

SOUTHERN BOG LEMMING

It is the lemmings found in Scandinavia that cycle in huge population explosions, resulting in mass migrations in which these small animals throw themselves into the ocean and thereby die. Because of this phenomenon, the lemming is a symbol of self-destruction.

An Eskimo legend tells how a tiny lemming outsmarted a wise owl. One day an owl saw a plump lemming eating outside its hole. He swooped down and told the lemming that two dog teams were heading in their direction. The lemming guessed what the owl was up to and said, "Owl, I'd rather be eaten by my neighbor than strangers. But before you eat me, let me sing so you can dance." The owl was pleased with the arrangement and gladly danced to the song of the lemming. The lemming kept singing, and when he saw his chance, he ran between the owl's legs and into his hole to safety.

COMMON NAME: Lynx

SCIENTIFIC NAME: *Felis lynx*

DESCRIPTION: The graceful lynx measures 34 to 42 inches in length, including a stubby 4-inch tail. The lynx is easy to identify because of the long tufts on its ears. The fur is a grayish tan with scattered spots on the legs. The feet are broad and fur covered, allowing for easy travel through snow.

HABITAT AND RANGE: Lynx are found in deep forests, swamps, and tundra throughout Canada and Alaska and in high mountainous areas south to Colorado. This same species is found in the forests of Europe and Asia. The lynx population depends on the population of its chief prey, the snowshoe hare, which seems to peak about every eleven years.

———

The name lynx is from the Greek word *leyssein*, meaning "to see," and refers to this animal's exceptional eyesight. The Greeks believed that these animals could see through solid objects. The mythological hero, *Lynceus*, had the power to see through anything. In heraldry, the lynx is symbolic of keen eyesight and prudence.

During medieval times it was believed that lynx urine solidifies into a precious stone called *ligurius*. This name was derived from *lync-urius*, or "lynx water." The process of solidification was thought to take seven days. A twelfth-century bestiary translated by T.H. White said that a lynx would go to great lengths to cover its urine: "When they have pissed the liquid, they cover it up in the sand as much as they can. They do this from a certain constitutional meanness, for fear that the piss should be useful as an ornament to the human race." The manner in which the lynx hid its urine proved to some people that it must have value.

In 1603 the Academy of the Lynxes was formed in Italy. The purpose of this school was to look for the truth and fight against superstition and ignorance. One of its earliest members was Galileo.

In Scandinavia and Germany, the lynx was considered sacred to Freya, the goddess of love, sex, and witchcraft. She is often pictured in a chariot pulled by two lynxes.

Some Native American tribes believed that the lynx was a keeper of secrets and a solver of mysteries. A folk saying adopting characteristics of the lynx to describe people is "suspicious as a lynx."

LYNX

COMMON NAME: Marmot, Yellow-bellied

SCIENTIFIC NAME: *Marmota flaviventris*

DESCRIPTION: The total length of this animal is 18 to 27 inches, including a 5- to 8-inch tail. It has the overall appearance of a fat woodchuck, but has yellowish markings and white on the muzzle and forehead. The ears are small and flat against the side of the head.

HABITAT AND RANGE: Found extensively in the Rocky Mountain regions in rocky slopes and valleys, north into Canada, and south to northern New Mexico.

SIMILAR SPECIES: The hoary marmot is similar in shape and size, but has light gray coloration and lives in the northern Rockies in Idaho, Montana, Washington, and north to Alaska. This species is sometimes called a Rockchuck.

The name marmot is from the French *marmontaine* or the Latin *musmontanus*, which means "the mouse of the mountain." The Alpine marmot, found throughout the Alps, was thought to be easy to tame. An account of this animal was published in a book on natural history in the 1830s and suggested that the marmot could be taught to dance and obey verbal commands.

Hoary marmots are also sometimes called whistlers from the loud whistling noise they make. Comte De Buffon wrote about this characteristic of marmots in his book *Histoire naturelle*, published in the eighteenth century:

"Whenever they venture abroad one is placed as a sentinel, standing high on an elevated rock, while the others amuse themselves in the fields below, or are employed in cutting grass, and making it into hay for their future convenience. And no sooner does their sentinel perceive a man, an eagle, a dog, or any other enemy, then he informs the rest by a kind of whistle, and is himself the last that takes refuge in the cell."

The marmot, the dog, and the mole were all considered meat that would greatly increase one's fertility.

YELLOW-BELLIED MARMOT

COMMON NAME: Marten, Pine

SCIENTIFIC NAME: *Martes americana*

DESCRIPTION: The head and body of this weasel-like animal measures 15 to 17 inches, the bushy tail another 9 inches. Though most of the fur is dark brown, lighter coloration is found on the chest, belly, and ears, including a buff or orange throat patch. It is similar to a mink but has a longer tail and is slightly larger and lighter in color.

HABITAT AND RANGE: This animal is found almost exclusively in coniferous forests throughout Canada, south to the Rocky Mountain states, and north to Alaska.

———

Aesop wrote that a marten was wandering about looking for food when she came upon a bronze foundry. She scurried inside and found a long, metal file and, not knowing any better, began to lick the file until her tongue was raw and bleeding. The poor marten believed her own blood was something from the file, so she kept licking until she had no tongue left.

Another Aesop's fable about the marten tells of a tanner who kept a white marten that ate only one mouse each day. One day the marten accidentally fell into the tanner's dye pot and instantly turned black. The mice believed that a change in color also meant a change in eating habits and concluded that the marten must no longer eat mice. Happy, they ran all over the floor until the surprised marten finally grabbed two mice and ate them. The rest scurried back to their holes, amazed at this mismatch of color and character. The moral? Things may look different, but don't count on them *being* different.

According to a Japanese Ainu mythology, both the marten and the raccoon were created to serve the bear. Both had black faces, indicating that they were cooks. Both these small animals were regularly offered for sacrifice.

PINE MARTEN

COMMON NAME: Mink

SCIENTIFIC NAME: *Mustela vison*

DESCRIPTION: Large weasel-like animals, mink measure 18 to 28 inches, including a long, rather narrow 6- to 9-inch tail. Males are noticeably larger than females. The rich, luxuriant fur is dark brown or black. A small amount of white occurs on the chin and throat.

HABITAT AND RANGE: Mink are never found far from fresh water and live along rivers and lakes throughout the United States with the exception of the Southwest, which is simply too dry for their needs. Today most mink used for the commercial fur trade are raised on farms.

Mink was an important character in many Native American mythologies. Most often Mink was seen as transformer/trickster, particularly among the people of the Pacific Northwest (though tribes found in the northern areas of this region more often portrayed Raven in this role). Mink was often carved into the totem poles of the region.

Mink was seen as clever, crafty, and, more often than not, erotic. It was said that he piled up the mountains and wherever he lay down to sleep, creeks and springs came up. Among his many feats, Mink was said to have killed monsters, stolen the sun, and changed the inhabitants of the early world to birds, beasts, and fish for the good of the human race that followed.

When portrayed as a trickster, Mink was often outwitted, but as a transformer he showed great powers. In one myth the mother of Mink was weaving in her hut with her back to the wall. The sun's rays touched her and impregnated her. She gave birth to Mink, whom she called Born-to-be-the-Sun. When Mink was still a child, he asked to go visit his father, the sun. The mother agreed, and Mink shot arrows to the sun until they became a chain he could climb.

When he reached the top, his father welcomed him, saying he was tired of walking back and forth across the sky every day. He asked Mink to do it for him, so the next morning Mink started off. By midday he became tired and, ignoring his father's instructions not to stop, brushed his aunts, the clouds, aside and lay down to nap. Immediately the sun shone too brightly. The earth began to burn, the trees burned off the tops of mountains, and huge cracks appeared in the earth. Father sun rushed to where Mink was and, in anger at his son's laziness, threw Mink back down to earth and resumed the daily journey himself.

The mink is actually a water-dwelling weasel. Putorius is the mink's scientific name, no longer used today. It means "stinker" and refers to the foul-smelling fluid

MINK

sprayed by the mink. The Cherokee tell the following story of why the mink smells: Mink was a terrible thief, and the animals soon tired of his thievery and decided to teach him a lesson. They built a large fire and threw Mink into it. When Mink began to smell like roasted meat, the animals decided that he had learned his lesson and would improve his behavior in the future, so they pulled him out of the fire. Unfortunately, Mink was burned black and still looks that way today. Whenever he becomes agitated or frightened, he once again smells like roasted meat. He never did learn his lesson—he's still a great thief.

According to an old folk saying, "You'd see more of the mink if he knew where the yard dog sleeps."

COMMON NAME: Mole, Eastern

SCIENTIFIC NAME: *Scalopus aquaticus*

DESCRIPTION: The eastern mole is tiny, measuring only 4 $^1/_2$ to 8 inches long, including a 1-inch naked tail. Dark (black, gray, or brown) velvety fur covers the body and the eyes. The paws are well adapted for digging.

HABITAT AND RANGE: Found in well-drained soils or grassy areas throughout the eastern half of the United States south of the Great Lakes area.

One of the principal tales of the Pueblo people was of the Middle Place, a mythical world where one could exist in peace and harmony with nature and other people. Middle Place served as an illustration of our inner calm and tranquility, traits the Pueblo admired and sought to achieve. One of the Pueblo myths about how people came to this place involved the small mole.

According to legend, in the beginning of time the world was all dark, and the people soon became tired of the blackness. One day a small mole appeared. He had burrowed his way through the darkness to the light above. The people became excited and asked the mole about his travels. The mole told them of a wonderful place that *felt* very different, but he could not tell them what it looked like because he was blind. The people decided they would go to see this new place, and they asked the mole to take them there. He agreed and began burrowing upward through the darkness. As the mole dug, he passed back the tiny pieces of dirt he removed, and the people dropped it behind them, so that their passageway was blocked and they could not return.

Suddenly they came out into a new place where the light was so brilliant that they became scared and wanted to run away. Because there was no way back, they eventually opened their eyes and saw the beautiful earth.

One of Aesop's fables tells of a young mole who bragged to his mother that, unlike other moles, he was able to see. The mother laughed and, to test him, gave him a lump of frankincense and asked him what it was. The young mole replied, "A pebble." His mother laughed again, saying that not only did he not have eyesight, he also lacked the sense of smell.

The Achomawi Indians tell why the mole is blind and has bent feet. One day the sun fell to the earth, and all the people ran away, afraid they would be burned by the sun. The animals ran also, all except for the little mole, who picked up the sun and said, "Don't run. We have to put the sun back in the sky."

The animals saw the little mole holding the sun up all by himself and ran to help. Together they were able to throw the sun back into the sky. Even so, the light of the sun burned the mole's eyes until he was

EASTERN MOLE

blind, and the weight of the sun bent his tiny fingers.

Medicine men and folk healers were thought to obtain great curative powers from the mole, the power transmitted to them in rituals. Throughout Europe, the mole has often been used as a folk medicine. Often the blood or flesh was rubbed into a patient's skin. Mole's blood was thought to cure epilepsy and drunkenness. Sometimes the mole's tiny paw was worn around the neck to cure epilepsy.

In France and England, the blood was thought to get rid of warts, and in Czechoslovakia the blood was put on the body to cure scrofula. A necklace made from a string dipped into mole's blood was sometimes placed around a child's neck to prevent bed-wetting.

An old southern folk saying is "Mole don't see w'at his nabor doin," meaning that if you bury yourself like the mole, you're going to miss what's going on.

The genus name *Scalopus* is from the Greek meaning "a foot for digging."

COMMON NAME: Moose

SCIENTIFIC NAME: *Alces alces*

DESCRIPTION: A massive animal, the moose weighs in at more than 1,200 pounds and stands $6^{1}/_{2}$ to 7 feet tall at the shoulders. The antlers are wide and spreading and can be up to $6^{1}/_{2}$ feet across. A fleshy dewlap is found on the throat, and the upper lip hangs over the bottom. The fur is dark brown.

HABITAT AND RANGE: Moose inhabit forests and thickets close to fresh water in the northern Rockies and throughout Canada and Alaska.

The name moose comes from the Algonquian word *moosu*, meaning "he strips bare" or "he eats off," a reference to the moose's habit of eating all the branches and bark from a tree.

The bull moose is a symbol of power. In 1912 Theodore Roosevelt adopted this animal as a symbol for the new political party. The moose is also considered a symbol of the balance between gentleness and strength.

In Russia and Scandinavia, moose have been trained to pull sleds and have even, on occasion, been broken to (very large) saddles.

Moose represents the northern region, considered the direction of wisdom. A Kutenai Indian legend says that the seasons are kept in mooseskin bags hanging in a tipi in a village in the very far north.

The Cree tell the following story of how people began to hunt moose: One night a family of moose were sitting around the fire when they suddenly smelled smoke from an Indian's pipe. The old bull and cow moose ignored the pipe, but the young bull moose took the pipe and smoked it. The old moose looked sadly at his son and said, "You have killed us all. Now the men will know where to find us."

The next day the men did, indeed, find the moose and killed the young bull, thanking him for smoking their pipe and giving his life so they could survive. They treated his spirit with great care. The next night the young bull moose woke up beside the old bull and cow and said that it was right to allow the men to hunt them. In the Cree tribe it was said that the hunters would always be successful if they showed the moose great respect.

The Wabanakis, who were descendants of the Algonquians, believed that the moose comes when it is called with a horn made of bark, either by blowing through the horn or by using the bark to scoop up water in the lake and allowing it to drip slowly as if a moose were drinking. The moose is attracted to the sound, believing it could be a mate.

According to Wabanakis legend, in the old days the moose was so large he could graze on the tops of the trees; he was also mean and destroyed the people, so they came

MOOSE

to fear him. The Great Spirit sent Ksiwham-beh, a culture hero, to the people to promise that he would change the moose. Ksiwham-beh made a horn out of birch bark and called the moose. When the moose came close, he pushed him again and again between his huge antlers until finally the moose shrank to the size he is now. Ksiwhambeh sent him off, telling him not to appear until he was called. Even today the moose rarely appears unless called by the hunter.

Native Americans considered the moose an omen of goodwill. They ate moose meat in the belief that it would give them the strength of the moose.

The hooves of the moose were at one time used to cure hundreds of afflictions. The left hind foot, for example, was used as a cure for epilepsy. Rings made from the antlers were used to cure headaches and dizziness, and the ground antlers, mixed with various herbs, were used as an antidote for snakebite. The genus and species names are from the Greek word *alke*, meaning "strength."

COMMON NAME: Mountain Goat
SCIENTIFIC NAME: *Oreamnos americanus*

DESCRIPTION: Mountain goats have shaggy white fur, dark hooves and horns, and an unmistakable bearded chin. They stand 3 to 3 1/2 feet tall at the shoulder and are 5 to 5 1/2 feet long from head to tail.

HABITAT AND RANGE: Usually staying high in mountain meadows, mountain goats are found only in the Rocky Mountains from southeastern Alaska south to Montana and northern Idaho.

The Scandinavian god, Thor, was said to have traveled in a chariot pulled by two goats, Tooth-gnasher and Gap-tooth. Legend says that one day Thor came to a farmer's house, where he decided to stop for the night. The farmer had little food, so Thor slew his own goats and served them for dinner, though he warned the farmer and his family not to eat any of the marrow from the bones.

After the meal Thor gathered the bones together again, raised his magic hammer over them, and restored them to life.

One of the oldest gods of Egypt, Khrum, was originally worshipped in the form of a ram or ram-headed man. Amun, another ancient Egyptian god, whose name meant "Invisible One," was god of the air. He adopted the ram with down-turned horns as his emblem because it was famed for its virility.

The goat in Greek and Roman mythology has varied folklore. The goat was always closely associated with the cult of Hera. According to legend, when Hera went to the woods to escape Zeus' anger, the goat gave away her hiding place. Because of this, youths threw spears at a she-goat during religious festivals honoring the goddess. In the cult of Athena, the goat was prohibited but was sacrificed once a year on the Athenian Acropolis.

Aphrodite rode a goat, and the animal was sacred to her. Also in Greek mythology, satyrs were mythical creatures that had certain characteristics of goats, and Pan, the Greek god of pastures, flocks, and shepherds, had the legs, horns, and beard of a goat. The wild goat was important to the Roman deities of Artemis and Dionysis.

In Christian Europe, goats were thought to have been friends of witches or the Devil (who combed the goats' beards once a day).

In addition to the Devil, the goat represents lust and sin in Christian symbolism, and Jesus is sometimes referred to as a scapegoat, taking away the sins of the world.

In South Africa goats were considered bringers of fertility and were connected with marriage. In Bulgaria goats were given as bridal gifts.

Early cultures held strange beliefs about goats, such as the superstition that they breathed through their horns or their ears.

Native Americans used goatskins to make bags used for carrying water.

The hides of mountain goats were prized by the Oglala Indians. Though the animals were seldom seen and thus the hides hard to

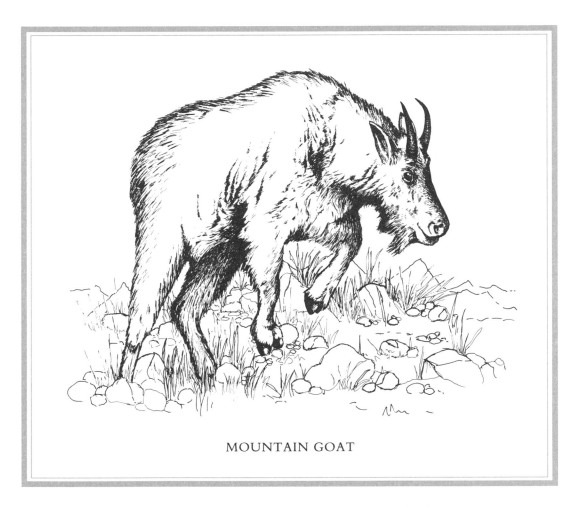

MOUNTAIN GOAT

come by, the Oglala sought after them because they were soft and pliable.

Because the goats were so adept at climbing steep, rocky paths, men who dreamed of mountain goats were thought to be able to easily climb up and down cliffs, and the earth would close up behind them, leaving no tracks.

In Burma, it was believed that goats cause eclipses by eating the sun or moon.

A Haitian Creole folk story says that one day Cat was teaching Goat to climb a tree. Goat was a slow learner, but day by day he learned more and more. One day Cat found Goat teaching Dog to climb a tree, too. Cat gave Goat no more tree-climbing lessons because if Dog could climb trees, too, Cat would have no place to hide.

The Cree word for the Rocky Mountain goat was *wapiti*, a word mistakenly used by English explorers to describe the elk. (See elk, page 36.)

In Chinese symbolism, the goat represents the solar yang, a masculine principle, and symbolizes peace.

The genus name *Oreamnos* is from Greek words *oros*, meaning "mountain," and *amnos,* meaning "lamb."

Native Americans from the Rocky Mountain regions considered mountain goat fat a great delicacy. It was sometimes even given as a gift.

COMMON NAME: Mountain Lion

SCIENTIFIC NAME: *Felis concolor*

DESCRIPTION: Tawny brown sleek fur covers this large wildcat. The tail is long and black tipped; underneath parts are pale. The mountain lion measures 5 to 9 feet in length, including a 2- to 3-foot tail. The head is relatively small for the large, strong body. Spots are found only on the very young.

HABITAT AND RANGE: Generally found only in the West, with isolated populations in the Appalachian mountains and in Florida. Mountain lions are adaptable to a wide range of habitats, including forests, deserts, and swamps.

SIMILAR SPECIES: The jaguar was once found as far north as Colorado but is now extremely rare in the United States.

Common American names for this cat include mountain lion in the Far West, puma or cougar in the Southwest, and panther, catamount, and painter in the East. The name catamount was a contraction for "cat of the mountain," an old name for the wildcat or mountain lion. The name cougar is said to have been a corruption of a name given to the cat by the Tupi Indians of South America. Because of the cat's tawny coat, they called it *suasuarana,* meaning "false deer." In translation this became *cuguacuarana,* and cougar came from this mistake.

The name panther is from the Sanskrit *pundarika,* meaning "tiger." Called panther or painter in the eastern woodlands, the mountain lion is an animal creator. The story is told that Panther wanted only day, and Chipmunk wanted only night. When night was made, Panther reached out and scratched Chipmunk's back in anger, and Chipmunk carries these claw marks to this day. (See Chipmunk page 28, which tells a variation of this story.)

Medieval European legend says that the panther slept in his den for three days and then emerged and emitted a mighty roar that all the animals heard. From his mouth came a sweet odor, which all animals liked except the dragon, who found it revolting. The dragon ran to his den and fell asleep, drugged by the odor of the panther's breath. This was taken in Christian symbolism to mean that the panther's breath was the Holy Spirit, who pleased everyone except the Devil, who ran to Hell where he belonged.

Medieval bestiaries suggested that the name panther came from the word *pan,* meaning "all" since Christ came to save all the world. Eventually the panther gained negative symbolism in Christianity and became representative of evil.

In European heraldry, the panther is

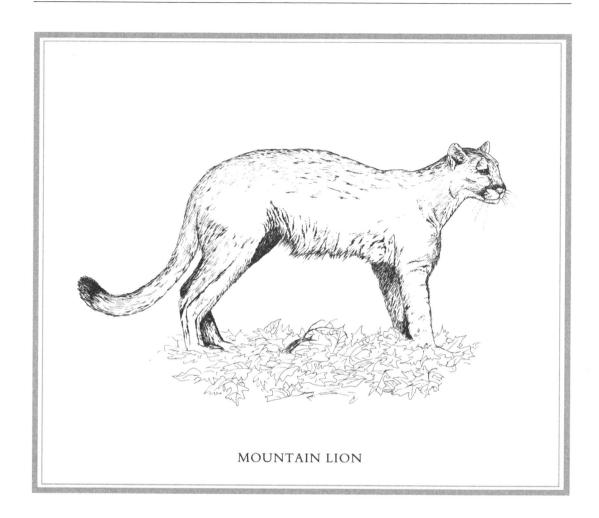

MOUNTAIN LION

shown as having the talons of an eagle, the tail of a lion, and flames coming from its head. It was representative of savage fury and remorselessness.

The panther was a sacred animal to Bacchus, the Roman god of wine, and was sometimes associated with the Egyptian god Osiris.

The Seneca Indians tell the story of a magical panther suit that made the wearer young and fearless and a great hunter. The mountain lion is often shown as a companion to Trickster, particularly among the Shoshone Indians. Among some California tribes he is shown as Coyote's elder brother.

COMMON NAME: Mountain Sheep

SCIENTIFIC NAME: *Ovis canadensis*

DESCRIPTION: The mountain, or bighorn, sheep is easily identified by its large, curved horns. The body is stocky and covered with light brown fur. It has a white rump and tail and stands 2 1/2 to 3 1/2 feet tall at the shoulder.

HABITAT AND RANGE: Mountain sheep are found in high mountain meadows and lightly wooded mountain slopes only in the western United States from northern British Columbia south into Mexico.

The mountain sheep was thought to have an uncanny knack for seeing around the rocks of the mountains. As one hunter put it, the bighorn can't hear thunder or smell a skunk, but it can see through rocks.

Native Americans used the wild sheep for meat and made the horns into utensils, weapons, and decoration. Some tribes piled mountain sheep horns in a ritualistic way, a monument used to trap evil spirits that were responsible for bringing bad weather.

The sun-ram was the symbol of the Egyptian god Amon of Thebes. It was also associated with other Egyptian deities such as Osiris, Qeb, and Shu. In Hindu mythology the ram was considered the steed of the fire-god Agni.

The ram has always been a symbol of masculine virility, and in Greece the ram was sacred to Zeus as the ram god of fertility.

The *shofar*, the Hebrew ritual horn, was made from a ram's horn.

In the early bestiaries, the ram symbolized spiritual leadership.

The ram was associated with the beginning of agriculture according to a Kabyle legend from northern Africa. In this region the ram is consulted about sowing and harvesting, and how and when festivals and feasts should be held.

In contrast to the strong and masculine symbolism of the ram, sheep became representative of timidity, helplessness, and silliness. Greeks sacrificed sheep to Zeus, Hera, and Mars. The Chinese prayed to the God of Sheep, Huang Ch'u-Ping, who could grant them large flocks. The Chinese consider the sheep a lucky animal and considered it a symbol of retirement.

Records from Southwest Asia dating around 9000 B.C. indicate that the sheep was the earliest domesticated animal.

A Yorkshire superstition stated that if you meet a flock of sheep on a journey, you will have good luck, especially if you walk through the flock. A North American Negro legend says that since the sheep didn't have enough sense to come out of the rain, God gave him a thick, wooly coat that sheds water.

MOUNTAIN SHEEP

The generally docile nature of sheep was referred to in the following European proverb: "He who makes himself a sheep, shall be eaten by the wolf." This proverb makes reference to responsibility: "Let every sheep hang by its own shank." This one remarks upon indulging in further wrongdoing: "One might as well be hanged for a sheep as for a lamb."

"A black sheep" was a term used to symbolize someone who was a disgrace to the family. Although the origin of the term is unknown, it has been in use since at least the end of the sixteenth century.

COMMON NAME: Mouse, House
SCIENTIFIC NAME: *Mus domesticus*

DESCRIPTION: Considered the most familiar rodent in North America, the little house mouse needs little introduction. The head and body measure 3 to 3 1/2 inches long, the naked tail is 2 to 4 inches long. The fur is dark brown, grayish, or black, and the small ears stand up from the head.

HABITAT AND RANGE: House mice are native to Asia but came into this country with the first explorers during the sixteenth century. Now this small rodent can be found throughout North America from Canada southward. Because food and nesting materials are readily available, the house mouse is most often found around human habitation.

The Winnebago Indians tell a delightful story about some mice who lived all their lives underneath a crooked log. Because they never ventured past the log, they believed they were the only creatures in the world. One day one of the mice stood up on his hind legs and stretched up as high as he could and just barely touched the bottom of the log. He thought he had touched the sky and sang this song:

> *Throughout the world*
> *Who is there like little me!*
> *Who is like me!*
> *I can touch the sky,*
> *I touch the sky indeed.*

> —From *The Indians' Book*, recorded and edited by Natalie Curtis

Because mice have been such an integral, though generally unwanted, part of our lives for centuries, much folklore and many folk sayings have sprung up about them. A Greek saying offers this advice, "In baiting a mouse-trap with cheese, always leave room for the mouse." Thomas Fuller wrote, "Burn not your house to fright away the mice." "Better a mouse in the pot than no flesh at all," is an Italian saying, and in regard to someone who shows foolhardy tendencies, one might say, "It is the bold mouse that breeds in the cat's ear."

A Greek tale tells how one day a lion caught a mouse, and the poor little mouse begged the lion to let him go, saying he really wasn't even a mouthful for the mighty lion anyway. The lion laughed and let the mouse go. Soon after, the lion was caught in a hunter's net and couldn't get out. The tiny mouse ran to him and gnawed through the ropes of the net to free the lion.

A fable from Aesop shows that the lion was not always so easygoing. One day a mouse woke up a sleeping lion by running over his mane and ears. The lion roared with anger and rushed around his den looking for the mouse. A fox, on seeing the commotion, misunderstood the lion and chided him for

HOUSE MOUSE

being afraid of a mouse. The lion replied that he was not afraid, but angry with the mouse for his ill breeding. The moral was that little liberties are sometimes seen as great offenses.

During medieval times, it was believed that a mouse held the soul of the dead. A German tale reflects this belief. Once a young servant girl fell asleep while shelling nuts. As she slept, her mouth opened and a tiny red mouse came out of her mouth and ran to the window. A man tried to wake the girl but could not, and he moved her to a different part of the room. When the mouse came back and could not find the girl, it became distraught and finally vanished, and at that instant, the girl died.

The Greek god Apollo, who was capable of sending plagues and dispelling the forces of the night, was symbolized by rats and mice.

Plautus, a Roman dramatist who lived from 254 to 184 B.C., wrote, "Consider the little mouse, how sagacious an animal it is which never entrusts its life to one hole only." Pliny, a Roman statesman, wrote *Natural History* in A.D. 77. In his book he suggests that children who wet the bed be fed boiled mice as a cure. Pliny also suggests that mouse ashes mixed with honey are good for an earache.

A sixteenth-century book entitled *Fourefooted Beastes* says that "Sodden mice are exceeding good to restraine and hold in the vrine of infants and children. . ."

Mice were also thought to be useful in curing whooping cough, fevers, chilblains, toothaches, and stammering.

The word mouse comes from the Sanskrit word *musha,* meaning "the thief."

COMMON NAME: Muskrat

SCIENTIFIC NAME: *Ondatra zibethicus*

DESCRIPTION: A muskrat is a round furry ball with a long, naked, flattened tail covered with scales. The total length, from nose to tip of tail, is 16 to 25 inches. This rodent has reddish brown hair on the back and light gray on the underparts.

HABITAT AND RANGE: Aquatic rodents, muskrats live in marshes, ponds, lakes, or slow streams. They are widespread throughout most of the United States and Canada with the exception of Florida and Georgia. Rather like small beavers, muskrats create lodges of grass and small sticks.

The northern Plains Indians tell that originally the world was a great womb and in this lived man and all the animals. When the womb broke, man jumped out first and this is why he is called Old Man and the animals are called Young Brothers.

The world was all under water and Old Man asked the beaver to dive underneath the water and bring back some mud. He tried, and the loon and the beaver tried, but no one could reach the mud. Then the little muskrat tried and was gone so long they feared he had drowned. He finally surfaced, holding a tiny fistful of mud. From this, Old Man made the earth and people.

The name muskrat was originally "musk cat," because of the musk glands found on the animal.

MUSKRAT

COMMON NAME: Ocelot

SCIENTIFIC NAME: *Felis pardalis*

DESCRIPTION: The beautiful dark-rimmed spots of this small wild cat make it easy to identify. The ocelot measures 3 to 4 1/2 feet from nose to tip of tail and weighs twenty to thirty-five pounds.

HABITAT AND RANGE: Ocelots are extremely rare in the United States and are seen only in Texas, Arkansas, Louisiana, and Arizona in wooded areas. They are more commonly seen in the southern part of the range that extends south to Paraguay.

———————

Ocelots are one of seven wild cats found in the United States. The others are the cougar, bobcat, lynx, jaguar, margay, and jaguarundi. All these wild cats are solitary, secretive, and difficult to see because they avoid human contact.

Cats both wild and domesticated have been essential figures in myth and folklore for centuries. According to Chinese legend, at one time cats ruled the world and could speak, whereas the first men were silent. One day a council of the wisest cats decided that ruling the world was just not worth the effort—they would rather lie in the sun. They gave men the power of speech and turned over the job of world rulers as well. Cats have been silently and happily basking in the sun ever since.

Cats have been seen as demonic beings in many cultures. A well-known Irish folktale tells of a cat who comes into the home of a fisherman. Only his wife and daughter are there, and the giant black cat scratches and terrifies the two women and eats all the fish in the house. The women hit the cat with a stick, but the cat seems unaware. Finally the wife runs away from the house, returning with a bottle of holy water, which she throws at the devil-cat. The cat disappears in a cloud of black smoke.

Aesop tells of a cat who falls in love with a young man and begs the goddess Aphrodite to turn her into a beautiful woman so she can be with the man. Aphrodite does so and watches as the two fall in love and run off to make passionate love together. Aphrodite, in a feisty mood, watches the lovers and, in the midst of their love-making, lets loose a small mouse. The young woman jumps from the bed and chases the mouse, and Aphrodite changes her back into a cat. (Moral: Even though you can change your form, you can't change your nature.)

Cats were revered by the Egyptians, and the death penalty was given to anyone who harmed a cat. When a cat died, an Egyptian family would shave off their eyebrows as a sign of mourning and would then have the cat mummified.

The goddess of the moon, Artemis, was often associated with the cat. She turned into a cat when the gods fled to Egypt, pursued by

OCELOT

Thyphon, a monster who tried to destroy all the gods. The eyes of the cat, which narrow and widen with changing light and mood, were said to do so like the waxing and waning of the moon.

The Greeks believed that cats were created by the moon, and clouds scuttling across the evening sky were thought to be mice running away from the moon-cat.

The ocelot was important in the mythology of Peru and was considered a totem animal in this culture. Because it hunts and lives near water, it is often depicted in association with the otter.

The superstition that cats have nine lives is one that has persisted since ancient times. It presumably refers to the cat's ability to land on its feet without injury, even from high places. In *Romeo and Juliet*, Shakespeare refers to this trait in the following lines:

Tybalt: *What wouldst thou have with me?*

Mercutio: *Good king of cats, nothing but one of your nine lives."*

The species name *pardalis* is from the Latin word *pardus*, meaning "a panther."

COMMON NAME: Opossum

SCIENTIFIC NAME: *Didelphis marsupialis*

DESCRIPTION: This nocturnal animal has a long, narrow white snout and a naked tail that measures 9 to 21 inches in length. The total length of the animal is 2 to 3 feet, and it can weigh up to fourteen pounds. The underfur is blackish and the outer hairs have a whitish tinge, making the animal appear grizzled.

HABITAT AND RANGE: Opossums can tolerate a wide range of conditions but prefer to live in wooded areas near water. Opossums were originally found only in the eastern United States, but they have been introduced to the West and are now common west of the Rocky Mountains, particularly along the coast.

A Cherokee folktale says that the opossum used to have a long, bushy tail and was very proud of it, and bragged about it all the time. Rabbit, who had no tail, became jealous and decided to play a joke on Opossum to teach him a lesson. The Great Animal Council held a dance to which all animals were invited. Rabbit went to tell all the animals and when he asked Opossum if he would be there, Opossum answered yes, if he could have a special seat to show off his tail. Rabbit said yes and promised to send someone over to comb out Opossum's beautiful tail to get it ready for the dance.

Rabbit then went to see Cricket and told him exactly how he wanted him to prepare Opossum's tail. Cricket agreed and went to Opossum's house. Opossum stretched out his long, bushy tail and closed his eyes in contentment as Cricket combed and worked on his tail. Cricket combed out the long, white hair and tied it all up with a red ribbon. Then he began snipping and cutting all the hair off the tail, still keeping it in place with the red ribbon.

Opossum went to the Great Council and when it was his turn to dance, he loosened the ribbon and stepped onto the dance floor. As he swung his tail back and forth, dancing proudly, all the hair fell off his tail until it was quite bare and naked. Everyone laughed, and Opossum turned and looked at his bare tail. He was so embarrassed and ashamed that he lay down and rolled over with a big, silly grin on his face—just as the opossum does today when taken by surprise.

A Southern version of how the opossum received his naked tail says that Opossum, Fox, and Rabbit were stealing corn from a cornfield near a graveyard. All of a sudden a ghost from the graveyard jumped out at them, and they ran away. Just as Opossum was climbing the fence, the ghost reached out and grabbed his tail, but Opossum kept going. The ghost was left with a handful of hair, and Opossum had a naked tail.

Another Cherokee legend tells how the opossum helped capture the sun. At the beginning all was darkness until finally the animals called a meeting and decided that

OPOSSUM

they must have light. The redheaded woodpecker said that he had heard there was light on the other side of the world. The animals were excited but could not decide who should go for the light.

Opossum, who had a beautiful bushy tail at that time, said he would go and he headed toward the east. Soon he began to see a light. The light became brighter and brighter, and his eyes began to hurt so he scrunched them shut. Even today the opossum's eyes are almost shut, and he only really opens them at night. Opossum kept going until he found the sun and took a small piece of it and hid it in his bushy tail.

The sun was hot and it began to burn his tail, but Opossum wouldn't let go. He traveled faster and faster and the piece of sun became

hotter and hotter until he finally returned home. He had brought light for all the animals, but at what a price! The sun had burned all the fur off his tail, and even today the opossum has a naked tail.

The name opossum is from the Algonquian word *apasoun*, meaning "white animal," and presumably refers to the opossum's grayish-white fur and white face and belly.

"Playing possum" refers to this animal's habit of going into a slight faint when faced with danger. Perhaps because of this trait, among Indians of the Amazon, the opossum is shown as the clever trickster.

A southern saying, indicating that you should use whatever gifts you were given, says, "a 'possum's tail is as good as a paw."

COMMON NAME: Otter, River

SCIENTIFIC NAME: *Lutra canadensis*

DESCRIPTION: Otter are generally seen in water. They have a long, weasel-like shape with dark fur and a yellowish sheen on the back of the shoulders and top of the head. The muzzle is blunt and the legs are short. A thick, furry tail, measuring 12 to 19 inches, narrows toward the tip.

HABITAT AND RANGE: River otters are found throughout almost all of the United States, including Alaska, and across Canada. They are not seen in southern Texas and desert areas of the southwest.

The name otter is thought to be from the Sanskrit *udra* or *udan*, meaning water. Pliny the Elder named the otter *Enhydris*, meaning "having to do with water."

To the Pawnee Indians the supreme animal power is the otter. Symbolic of wisdom, the otter is believed to be the wisest of all animals. The Winnebago Indians also believed in the wisdom of the otter, and their medicine men relied upon its guidance. Pouches made from otter skin were used by the medicine men to hold their medicines and charms. Some tribes believed that the otter symbolized feminine energy and the power of water.

Otters have long been hunted for their fine fur. North American Indians often used it for ceremonial paraphernalia. They made it into medicine sacks for special occasions. Older men wrapped strips of the fur around their braids. Otter fur in a chief's headdress was symbolic of wisdom.

European otters were said to have been kept at the Swedish court for the purpose of catching fish for the king's table.

In true "Bre'r Rabbit and the Tar Baby" style, stories are told of how Otter would be caught and would beg not to be thrown into the water. His pursuers would laugh and do just that, and then Otter would laugh last as he swam away gracefully. It was believed that Otter helped dead souls across the lake to the spirit world.

Ainu Indians tell the story that Otter was asked to create Fox and was told to make him red. Otter forgot and made him white, but the foxes complained until Otter finally rubbed salmon roe over Fox and colored him red.

One tale says that once, a very long time ago, all the animals in the forest decided to hold a contest to see who had the most beautiful coat of all. Though all believed that the otter would win the contest, no one was sure he would even come because he was a lonely animal and rarely came down river to see the other animals.

Rabbit was excited about the contest and wanted to win it so badly that he thought of a plan. He offered to travel up the river to tell

RIVER OTTER

Otter of the contest. All the animals agreed.

When Rabbit came to Otter's house, Otter agreed to go back with him and they started on their journey. On the way down the trail, Rabbit told Otter that it often rained fire in this part of the world and when they stopped for the night, he had best take his coat off so it wouldn't get burned. Otter did this and when he was sound asleep that night, Rabbit threw coals up in the air and cried, "It's raining fire!" Otter jumped in the river without his coat.

Rabbit stole the coat and went quickly to the council in his new coat, but the other animals knew him anyway. He tried to run away, but Bear grabbed his tail. Rabbit kept running and his tail broke off, and that's why he has such a short tail today. Otter got his coat back, but stayed in the river, and Rabbit got a stubby tail for all of his troubles.

It was once believed that if you were possessed by an otter, or if you ate otter meat or even a fish killed by an otter, you would lose your memory. If this happened, a tight band was sometimes tied around the person's head to keep the otter from coming into the brain.

A dried otter heart was thought to be a cure for cholera.

COMMON NAME: Porcupine

SCIENTIFIC NAME: *Erethizon dorsatum*

DESCRIPTION: Porcupines are easy to identify, particularly when they are frightened and their quills stand on end. Total body length including the tail is 2 to 3 feet. It is the only mammal in North America that is covered with spiny quills.

HABITAT AND RANGE: Porcupines live in forested areas throughout western and northern North America, south to Pennsylvania in the east.

———

The genus name is from Latin words meaning "having a back that irritates." The name porcupine is from the Latin *purcus,* meaning "pig," and *spina,* meaning "thorn." Porcupines are also commonly called hedgehogs. In his play *Macbeth,* Shakespeare refers to this small animal as "Hedge-pig."

The porcupine was seen as a companion to the trickster Coyote in many western American Indian tales. Two tales, Coyote and Porcupine and Beaver and Porcupine, are well-known.

Porcupine is often seen as controlling cold, as he does in the tale of Beaver and Porcupine. Beaver plays a trick on Porcupine by taking him to the middle of the lake and leaving him there. Porcupine sings a magic song that causes the lake to freeze, and he walks on the ice to the shore. He gets back at Beaver by taking him to the top of a tree and leaving him there.

In Hausa Negro folklore, Porcupine is portrayed as having power over witches and people in this world and in the next.

Aristotle wrote that the hedgehog could forecast a change in the wind. Another ancient belief about this animal was that he used his quills to protect himself in case of a fall from a great height. In Christian symbolism the hedgehog represented evil and sin, but in other cultures it was a symbol of the Great Mother.

The porcupine's normal method of defense is to roll up into a ball and sit still, protected by its spines. The quills were sought after by hunters who used them to treat and soften skins. In addition, in some religious orders, hedgehog hides were worn next to the skin as an alternative to the hair shirt. According to legend, the hedgehog would sometimes, out of spite, urinate over its own spines, which would cause them to rot and fall out and be useless for men.

It was commonly believed that the porcupine could fight from close in or at a distance, shooting his quills when his enemy was far away. Because of this belief, the Duke of Orleans in 1397 instituted the Order of the Porcupine and adopted the motto *cominus et eminus,* which means "coming and going."

One proverb suggests that "a hedgehog lodges among thorns, because they, them-

PORCUPINE

selves, are prickly." Another tells us that "there is no rape among porcupines."

In England the porcupine was disliked by farmers, who believed that they would milk their cows at night. Another English superstition was that the porcupine carried apples on its spines. The same is true in Greece, though the fruit was grapes, not apples.

One story says that the hedgehog gathered grapes by knocking them off the vine and then rolling on its back to capture them on its spines. The porcupine then brought the grapes to its young.

One of the first of Aesop's fables was of the fox and the hedgehog, the moral of which dealt with people embezzling from the state. A fox crossing a river swam by mistake into a narrow creek and became trapped in the shallow water. His predicament was made even worse when hungry horseflies covered his body.

A hedgehog walked by and asked the fox if he would like him to drive away the flies. The fox declined the offer, saying that these flies were almost full. If they were driven away, hungry new ones were sure to take their place and drink his blood until none was left.

The peculiar noise made by a porcupine, something between snoring and hard breathing, has given rise to different superstitions. It has been suggested that ghosts or evil spirits may be around when this sound is heard.

The jawbone was sometimes hung around a child's neck for protection from the evil eye. Blood from the hedgehog was thought to be good for getting rid of warts. The gall bladder was used for deafness, and the fumes from burnt bristles was considered a general antidote, good for human and beast alike.

In Morocco pounded and roasted porcupine liver was given to school boys to help them remember their lessons. In England the left eye fried in oil was a remedy for insomnia during the seventeenth century. Eating the flesh was forbidden among people in Madagascar, particularly warriors, so they would not curl up in fright when attacked.

Members of the women's quillwork guild among the Plains Indians decorated ceremonial robes with porcupine quills. Before beginning her work, a woman had to fast and pray and had to retain a contemplative attitude as she worked with brightly dyed quills.

Among this tribe, the porcupine was connected to the sun and was considered a manifestation of the Creative Principle. The quills, which she laid out in a traditional geometrical pattern, were considered rays of sun and thus sacred. The quillworker, who has trapped the sun, understood the spirituality of the garment, which is now useful for both the maker and wearer.

COMMON NAME: Prairie Dog, Black-tailed
SCIENTIFIC NAME: *Cynomys ludovicianus*

DESCRIPTION: Not a dog at all, this large rodent measures 13 to 26 inches in length, including a 2- to 4-inch tail. The fur is yellowish brown, pale underneath. The tail has a distinctive black tip.

HABITAT AND RANGE: Prairie dogs at one time created colonies or towns that covered several square miles. Today their numbers have been greatly reduced, and their colonies are much smaller. They live in shortgrass prairies of the Midwest.

The genus name *Cynomys* is from the Greek name *kynos*, which means "dog." Prairie dogs were described in 1541 by the Spanish explorer Francisco Coronado. His writings compared them to ground squirrels. Nearly 200 years later, Louis and Francois Verendrye saw these short-legged little creatures and called them *petits chiens*, or "little dogs." In their journals, Lewis and Clark referred to them as barking squirrels.

Prairie dogs are portrayed as friendly animal actors in the mythologies of the Plains and Southwestern Indians. Sometimes the prairie dog is described as a harbinger of rain, with the power to lead people to water.

During the late nineteenth century, it was estimated that prairie dog communities covered more than 600,000 square miles and were occupied by five billion prairie dogs.

BLACK-TAILED PRAIRIE DOG

COMMON NAME: Rabbit, Eastern Cottontail

SCIENTIFIC NAME: *Sylvilagus floridanus*

DESCRIPTION: The eastern cottontail weighs 1½ to 4 pounds, and measures 12 to 19 inches, including a short 2-inch cotton puff tail. The fur is brownish above, white below. The ears are long and tapered, standing straight up from the head.

HABITAT AND RANGE: The eastern cottontail is found in several different kinds of habitats, including grassland, woods, and farmlands throughout eastern North America and in parts of the Southwest and Pacific Northwest.

SIMILAR SPECIES: Other well-known species include the snowshoe hare, *Lepus americanus*, which is rusty brown in summer and white in winter, with black-tipped ears and nose. The white-tailed jackrabbit, *Lepus townsendii*, is common on the Great Plains and prairies. It is larger than the cottontail, weighing five to seven pounds, and is grayish brown above. The antelope jackrabbit has very large ears, measuring almost 7 inches.

The rabbit is one of the most important trickster animals, particularly in the southeastern United States and in the Great Basin states. In the southeast, he is also seen as a great benefactor to humankind. For example, he goes across the ocean to get fire to give to humans.

The Mohawk Indians tell the following tale of how their people learned the rabbit dance. Several hunters were out in the woods and they saw a very large rabbit. They did not shoot it but waited to see what would happen. The rabbit saw them but did not run away. Instead, he carefully lifted one leg and thumped the ground.

Other rabbits heard the thump and they came running to the clearing. The big rabbit began to thump a rhythm on the ground with his foot, and the other rabbits made a circle around him and began to dance in and out. After the rabbits danced for a bit, the big rabbit thumped one more time and then, in a single giant leap, jumped over the hunters and disappeared.

The hunters returned to their camp and taught the dance to the others in the tribe, and for many, many years the men and women of the tribe did the rabbit dance in gratitude to the rabbit for the many gifts it gave them.

Many of the southeastern folktales about rabbits are of African or European origin. In African folklore, particularly in Nigeria, Rabbit is seen as trickster, along with Spider, Tortoise, and Chevrotain. Uncle Remus' Bre'r Rabbit tales are famed examples of these trickster stories.

A hare is a long-eared relative of the rabbit. The Algonquian tribes of eastern North America credited the great white hare with

EASTERN COTTONTAIL RABBIT

forming the earth and ordering and enlarging it. The culture hero first appeared as Hare and was a chief actor in many trickster tales.

In Europe (especially in Ireland, Wales, and Scotland) during the Middle Ages, it was commonly believed that witches could turn themselves into hares. Thus, it was bad luck if a hare crossed one's path. This bad luck could be reversed by retracing one's steps. During the sixteenth century this superstition was so commonly accepted that on May Day, if a hare was found among the herd, it was hunted and killed, for it was believed to be a witch. If the rabbit runs behind you, you will have good luck. During the nineteenth century, country people in England refused to eat hares, believing the souls of their grandmothers had entered into them.

According to a Buddhist legend, a hare sacrificed its life to appease Buddha's hunger, and as a reward Buddha sent him to the moon, where he sits now. In Aztec mythology the moon was once as bright as the sun, until the sun threw a hare in the face of the moon and darkened it. In Egypt a rabbit was a symbol of the moon, and a Hindu legend tells of a rabbit sitting in the lap of the moon god.

Aesop's fable of the tortoise and the hare is one of his most famous. The two animals run a race. Sure of winning, the hare lies down and takes a nap before he reaches the goal. He oversleeps and is passed by persevering tortoise, who wins the race. This story is often told throughout the world.

According to these old folk sayings, one can't "run with the hare and hunt with the hounds," and one must remember that "if you run after two hares, you will catch neither."

The phrase "As mad as a March hare" was made famous with the hare in Lewis Carroll's Alice in Wonderland.

The term harelip refers to a cleft in the upper lip which resembles the configuration of the hare's upper lip. Pregnant women were advised not to look at a hare, for fear the child would be born with a harelip.

Romans never killed rabbits for food, but they did use them for divination. Christians, also, did not eat rabbits or hares, as evidenced in Deuteronomy 14: 7–8, "Ye shall not eat . . .

the hare and the coney . . . they are unclean unto you."

Fishermen believe if anyone mentions a rabbit, the catch will be poor, and miners think that to see a hare on the way to the mine will bring bad luck. Actors sometimes put on stage makeup with a rabbit's foot or rub a rabbit's foot on their face and hands for luck on the opening night of a play.

Carrying a rabbit's foot was thought to bring good luck, and it was customary for a mother to brush a newborn's face with a rabbit's foot, thus assuring a lifetime of luck for the child.

Saying "rabbit" three times before going to sleep on the last day of the month is supposed to bring good luck, as will saying "white rabbit" early in the morning on the first day of each month.

The rabbit was originally associated with Easter as a fertility symbol. The word Easter is derived from the name of the pagan goddess of spring, Eostre. In Greek mythology, the rabbit was sacred to the goddess Aphrodite and also was a symbol of fertility. To eat rabbit meat was thought to promote fertility. The Roman scholar Pliny suggested that eating rabbit meat would keep one from being barren. During the Middle Ages, the image of a rabbit was sometimes included on a wedding ring to insure that the couple would be fertile.

COMMON NAME: Raccoon

SCIENTIFIC NAME: *Procyon lotor*

DESCRIPTION: Raccoons are easy to identify because of the characteristic mask on the face and the black-ringed tail. These animals weigh from eight to nineteen pounds and measure 2 to 3 feet in length, including a 7- to 16-inch tail.

HABITAT AND RANGE: Raccoons have adapted well to living near humans and often live in suburban areas. They must live near water and are found abundantly along wooded streams. These animals are found throughout the United States except for some areas in the Rocky Mountains, north into central Canada, and south throughout Mexico.

The beautiful markings on a raccoon's face and its peculiar living habits have given it many common names, including mask wearer, fish-catcher, crab-eater, night-rover.

Raccoons are often portrayed as trickster, but never as transformer or creator animals. Even as a trickster, it is different from other trickster animals in that it is never portrayed as foolish and is rarely the brunt of a joke. Many cultures considered the raccoon magical or even sacred. The Sioux Indians called it "one who is sacred," or "one with magic," presumably because of the black mask. The Dakota Sioux called it *wee-kah teg-alega*, meaning "sacred one with painted face." The Aztecs called it "she who talks with gods," and "little one who knows things."

The name raccoon is from the Algonquian word *Ah-rah-koon-em*, meaning "hand scratcher." This name is popular and appears in many languages including Dutch, German, Swedish, Portuguese, and Spanish.

A Nez Percé legend describes how the raccoon received its unusual markings. A long time ago all the animals had soft brown fur and all looked alike. During this time, Coyote and Raccoon were always playing tricks on each other. One day Coyote was sound asleep by the river, and Raccoon crept up and, for a trick, was going to tie Coyote's tail to a vine. Just as Raccoon came close, Coyote grabbed him and swung his tail back and forth through the hot embers of the fire until Raccoon's tail had rings of brown from the mud and black from the fire.

Raccoon cried out, "Stop!" and Coyote, in the confusion, grabbed Raccoon's ear to get his tail out of the fire and dropped him headfirst into the hot coals.

Raccoon cried out again, "It's hot, it's hot," and Coyote, not really meaning to hurt his friend, grabbed handfuls of cool white mud from the riverbank and threw them at Raccoon's eyes. When finally everything had calmed down, Raccoon's face had a black and

RACCOON

white mask, and it has remained that way to this day.

A Caddo legend tells how the raccoons can tell just when the persimmons are ripe on the tree. This is a wonderful gift, for if persimmons are picked a day too early, they are sour enough to make one's mouth pucker, and if picked a day too late, they're too mushy to eat.

The legend says that one day a man was called by the Great Spirit to take a journey. When one is called by the Great Spirit, one must leave at once and not stop to eat or drink, for this is a journey of the spirit, not the body. This particular man was, perhaps, not quite ready to take a spiritual journey, for when he came to a grove of persimmon trees, he could see that they were perfect for eating, and he couldn't resist them. He stopped and ate his fill, and the Great Spirit was angry and told the man he would never complete the

spiritual journey because he had disobeyed.

The Great Spirit said that the man would spend the rest of his days scurrying around the earth as a small, furry creature. The man begged and pleaded, but the Great Spirit was firm. He turned the man into a raccoon, which today leaves a footprint like a human, uses his hands like a man, and has the ability to always know when the persimmons are ripe for picking.

Folk healers often used the fat from raccoons on sprains and bruises and sometimes cooked with raccoon fat in place of lard. Raccoon fat was also useful in softening leather. Raccoon coats, popular during the 1920s, required fifteen skins each, and for a while raccoon populations were greatly reduced. Luckily this fad did not last long.

A "coon's age" means any length of time beyond what is considered normal.

COMMON NAME: Shrew, Long-tailed

SCIENTIFIC NAME: *Sorex sp.*

DESCRIPTION: Long-tailed shrews are generally brownish black with white underneath. The long snout is reddish, and the tail measures one third to one half the total length of the body (up to 6 1/2 inches long.) Species look very much alike and are difficult to tell apart.

HABITAT AND RANGE: Shrews seem to be found in almost every kind of habitat—tundra, desert, grassland, rivers, and swamps.

Pliny suggested in his *Natural History* that the bite of a shrew-mouse was venomous. In Shropshire, England, it was believed that if you met a shrew while setting off on a journey, you would have bad luck. In other areas of England, it was believed that you could avoid bad luck if you crossed your feet when you saw a shrew.

In a 1579 book called *Thousand Notable Things,* it was stated that if a shrew crosses over any part of a beast, that part will become lame. Likewise in Dorset, it was thought that

LONG-TAILED SHREW

if a shrew ran over a man's foot, he would become crippled. The shrew, however, also faced risks, according to superstition. If a shrew fell into a rut made by a cart wheel, it was believed that the shrew would die.

A folk cure for rheumatism was to carry a dead shrew in one's pocket.

The word shrew sometimes refers to a woman of an unpleasant nature. This presumably refers to the voracious appetite and sharp, ugly features of this small rodent. The most famous shrew was the one tamed by William Shakespeare in *Taming of the Shrew*. A proverb referring to this type of woman is, "Every man can rule a shrew save he that has her."

The shrew is considered sacred in Egypt.

COMMON NAME: Skunk

SCIENTIFIC NAME: *Mephitis mephitis*

DESCRIPTION: The skunk is black except for a large white stripe that goes from nose to tail. The tail is long and very fluffy, measuring 6 to 15 inches long. The total length, including the tail, is 20 to 30 inches.

HABITAT AND RANGE: Skunks are adaptable and are at home in woodlands, farmlands, deserts, and suburban areas throughout most of the United States, southern Canada, and northern Mexico.

The scientific name *Mephitis mephitis* is from the Latin name for a poisonous vapor coming from the ground. The common name is thought to come from the Abnaki Indian name, *segonky,* meaning "he who urinates."

The skunk is also called a polecat, presumably from an old French word meaning "fowl" or "hen," since the skunk often raids the henhouse. Uncle Remus tells the following tale about this little mammal. When the weather "wuz gittin' kinder shivery," Bre'r Polecat decided he had better find a warm place to stay. He went walking through the woods until he came to a hollow tree where Bre'r Rattlesnake had a warm house. He called out to Bre'r Rattlesnake to let him in, but Mr. Rattlesnake wouldn't do it.

Bre'r Polecat said that he was a good housekeeper, and Bre'r Rattlesnake said it was easy to keep other folks' house and that there was no room for him. Bre'r Polecat said shoo, everybody made room for him, but Mr. Rattlesnake said no and after a while Bre'r Polecat "went pacin' off somers else."

The Oglala Sioux associated skunks with mysterious earth powers, similar to those attributed to the badger. Skunks were well respected because, when fighting, they showed a "no flight" quality. Dakota chiefs

SKUNK

had skins of skunks tied to their heels to symbolize the fact that in battle they were like the skunk and never ran away.

The Cherokee believed that the scent of the skunk would keep away contagious diseases. A "scent bag" holding the noxious odor was hung over the doorway, and a small hole pierced through the bag so the scent would permeate the room. If the epidemic was particularly bad, as in the smallpox epi-demic of 1866, the entire body of the skunk was hung up, the meat cooked and eaten, and skunk oil rubbed over the skin.

Though the odor of the skunk may not contain natural chemicals that can combat contagious diseases, the fact that the odor greatly discouraged visits from those who may be infected helped to stop the spread of disease, making the stench of the skunk effective in its own way.

COMMON NAME: Squirrel, Gray

SCIENTIFIC NAME: *Sciurus carolinensis*

DESCRIPTION: This small animal has gray fur with a large, bushy tail measuring 8 to 9 inches long. From the nose to the tip of the tail is 17 to 19 inches. Underparts are whitish or sometimes rusty orange, and the tail generally has darker markings. Ears are small and erect.

HABITAT AND RANGE: Very common throughout the eastern half of the country, the gray squirrel inhabits broad-leaved forests and suburban areas.

The western gray squirrel, *Sciurus griseus,* is found along the Pacific coast from the Mexican border to Canada. The chattering, busy squirrel has given rise to much folklore. A common folk belief was that if a squirrel stores large quantities of nuts in autumn, the following winter will be a severe one. The name squirrel is derived from two Greek words, *skia,* meaning "shade," and *oura,* meaning "tail," and is loosely translated as "he sits in the shade of his own tail."

Medb, an Irish goddess, chose the squirrel and the bird as her emblems.

A Cherokee superstition forbids those suffering from rheumatism from eating squirrel meat, since the small gray squirrel hunches over in a cramped position while eating. In the southern United States, Indian women who were responsible for planting groundnut crops were not allowed to eat squirrel meat for fear this would cause the crops to dry up and die.

A Russian folktale is told about the squirrel and the lion. The squirrel agreed to serve the lion and to meet all his needs in return for a wagonful of nuts. For years the squirrel was at the lion's beck and call, but the lion never got around to getting the nuts for the squirrel. The squirrel did not want to leave without receiving his payment, but he was scared to ask for it from the lion.

After years of faithful service from the squirrel, the lion finally decided to let him go and, true to his promise, gave him a wagonful of magnificent nuts. The problem was that the poor old squirrel had lost his teeth years before, and the nuts were now useless to him.

A child's superstition says that if you see a squirrel on the way to school, you should watch which way it runs. If it goes to the right, you will learn your lessons well that day; if it goes to the left, you will not learn as quickly. A New England variation of this superstition says that if a squirrel crosses your

GRAY SQUIRREL

path from left to right, you will have bad luck. If it crosses from right to left, your luck will be good.

Scandinavian legend tells us that the squirrel lives in the Tree of Life and is symbolic of spitefulness and mischief. In Norway, squirrels are called the postmen of the forest because they jump from tree to tree carrying messages. The squirrel appeared on a Norwegian coin issued in 1958.

COMMON NAME: Weasel, Long-tailed
SCIENTIFIC NAME: *Mustela frenata*

DESCRIPTION: True to its name, the tail of this small animal is almost as long as the body and measures 3 1/2 to 7 inches long. The head and slender body are approximately 7 1/2 to 15 inches long. The tail is black at the tip, the body mostly brown with pale underside. Males are twice as big as females.

HABITAT AND RANGE: Living in most parts of the United States except parts of the Southwest, the long-tailed weasel adapts to a wide range of habitats, including forests, marshes, and farmlands, but will almost always stay close to water.

In *Hesitant Wolf and Scrupulous Fox*, edited by Karen Kennerly, the story is told of a man who trapped a weasel, tied her up, and carried her to the river to drown her. The weasel begged the man not to kill her, telling him that she would be good for his house— that she would eat the mice and lizards who ate his food. The man hesitated, then agreed that it was true she would eat the mice and lizards. But he next pointed out that the weasel would eat all the food the mice and lizards would have eaten, anyway, so he'd be no better off.

The name weasel is from an Anglo-Saxon word, *wsule*, meaning "savage and bloodthirsty." From this meaning comes the habit of calling a sly and dangerous person a weasel.

The white fur found on weasels during winter months is called ermine. This name is from the Latin *mus armenius*. The Reverend Thomas Bankes wrote in *Universal Geography* in 1790 that ermine was "the softest and most beautiful of all furs. . . ." To have such beauty is not always a great advantage, though, as is

indicated by the proverb, "In an ermine, spots are soon discovered."

Nevertheless, the ermine is a symbol of purity. One European superstition suggested that an ermine would rather be captured than to become muddy while trying to escape. Ferdinand I, king of Naples in the fifteenth century, adopted as his motto, *Malo mori quam foedari*, "better to die than to be sullied," and included a white ermine in a circle of mud on his banner. Whenever ermine fur was included on ceremonial robes, it indicated that the wearer was someone of great personal integrity.

All three species of weasels found in North America will kill more game than they can eat. John James Audubon wrote in 1785 that "this little Weasel is fierce and bloodthirsty, possessing an intuitive propensity for destroying every animal and bird within its reach. . . ."

The Roman statesman Pliny the Elder says that the weasel eats rue to make himself immune to snake bites.

LONG-TAILED WEASEL

It is considered unlucky to meet a weasel in Ireland, for these animals were thought to be descendants of "Danes cats," and their bite and spit were considered poisonous. Similarly, in Bohemia the look of a weasel is thought to blind or blight you. In Germany, however, to see a weasel on the roof meant good luck.

In some areas, farmers believed the weasel's bite was poisonous and could kill cattle, but they did not kill these small mammals for fear that hundreds of weasels would come to avenge another weasel's death. It was customary on Saint Matthew's Day, September 21, or Saint Catherine's Day, November 25, to hold a festival for the weasels to keep them away from the cattle.

In medieval times, the weasel was thought to be able to bring the dead back to life. It was a commonly held superstition that the weasel conceived through her ear and brought forth young from her mouth, and thus became symbolic of the formation of speech. It also became a symbol of prudence and fortification against enemies.

The implication that the weasel and the cat display unpleasant characteristics is shown in the proverb that says, "When the weasel and the cat make a marriage, it is a very ill presage."

According to American Indians, the weasel can hear everything that is said and has prophetic powers. For example, the weasel is thought to have told of the white man's coming and of the resulting destruction.

The weasel in the popular children's song, "Pop Goes the Weasel," does not refer to the animal but was a term applied to those who frequented taverns.

ERMINE

COMMON NAME: Wolf, Gray

SCIENTIFIC NAME: *Canis lupus*

DESCRIPTION: The wolf is a large doglike animal measuring 53 to 71 inches, including a long, bushy tail. The fur is generally gray but is sometimes almost black or silvery gray.

HABITAT AND RANGE: The gray wolf was at one time found over much of North America and Eurasia but is now confined to Asia and to Alaska, Canada, and isolated pockets in the Rockies and Great Lakes region. Wolves inhabit forest and tundra areas.

———

Wolves are both revered and feared wherever they are found and almost always provoke much controversy. Wolves have been considered symbols of both night and day, death and life-giver, darkness and sun. In her book *Women Who Run with the Wolves*, Clarissa Estés tells the story of La Loba, Wolf Woman, whose work it is to collect and preserve all that is in danger of being lost.

La Loba lives in the mountains and the desert looking for the bones of wolves, and as she finds them, she assembles an entire skeleton until finally when the last bone is in place, she begins to sing over the bones. As she sings, the skeleton begins to flesh out until the creature begins to breathe and finally jumps up and runs away. If a bit of magical moonlight or a stray sun ray touches this wolf, it will turn into a laughing woman.

In North American woodland mythology, Wolf is most often depicted as brother of the culture hero, Nanabozho. In these stories, Wolf is killed, only to be revived to rule over the country of the dead. In other myths, Wolf and Coyote are brothers or partners.

Some American Indian peoples saw Wolf as friend and teacher and thought that wolves were represented by Sirius, the Dog Star, believed to be home of the gods. The Shoshone believed that at the death of the body the soul went to the land of the wolf. The Nez Percé believed that all people were descendants of the wolf. In the Pacific Northwest, the Wolf Society was a doctoring society formed when the transformer killed the wolf and danced in his skins, thus attaining the power to cure.

The Pawnee were one of the most famous of all the western tribes. The name Pawnee means "wolf" and was given to this tribe because their method of warfare resembled characteristics of the wolf. Like the wolf, the Pawnees seemed tireless.

Arapaho scouts who went ahead of the war party to spy on the enemy were called wolves because, like this animal, they "prowled about the enemy's camp, moving by night and falling on the foe unawares," according to a description in *The Indians' Book,* edited by Natalie Curtis.

The East Cree Indians saw Wolf as a creator and tell this tale: The trickster Wisagatcak built a dam across the river to catch the giant beaver. Just as Beaver came, though, a muskrat bit Wisagatcak, who then missed his target. The beavers were so angry that the trickster tried to catch one of them that they allowed all the waters to flow until the earth was covered and everything began to drown.

Muskrat tried to dive underneath the water to find the earth, but he drowned. Raven went out looking for land, but he could not see any of the earth. Finally Trickster called on Wolf for help. Wolf swam around and around a raft with a ball of moss in his mouth. The moss grew and grew until earth formed on it. Wolf put it down, and the animals danced around it, singing down powerful spells until finally the moss grew to make the earth.

Because the wolf is a fast runner and capable of great endurance, scouts of the Oglala Sioux wore wolf hides so they would absorb these characteristics. The Oglala saw the strength of the wolf pack and banded together to increase their own strengths.

Wolves have always been wanderers and are thought to have great knowledge. Wolf songs were taught in dreams or visions, and these, as well as the actual howl of the wolf, were thought to have special powers. According to a Dakota Sioux legend, a wolf taught man a song, and when he howled, wind was created. When he howled again, fog appeared. Both of these were useful to the warrior since wind served to confuse enemy and fog helped one to be invisible.

In Roman legend the twins Romulus and Remus were sons of the god Mars and a mortal woman. When they were born, the king became jealous of their potential power and ordered that they be put in a basket and thrown into the river to die. The basket floated downstream and a she-wolf found them and suckled them. They were brought up by a poor shepherd and later founded the city of Rome. Since this time, the wolf has been the emblem of Rome.

A Latin saying states that "The wolf changes his coat, but not his nature." A similar Russian saying is, "No matter how much you feed a wolf, he will always return to the forest."

An old proverb says, "As a wolf is like a dog, so is a flatterer like a friend." A second proverb says, "The wolf might lose his teeth but never his nature," and a third states, "Who keeps company with the wolf, will learn to howl." The phrase "Keep the wolf away from the door" means to earn enough money to keep the bill collectors away.

It was commonly believed in many cultures that the devil himself took the shape of a wolf, and it was thought that wolves had the power to paralyze victims and strike them dumb. If you've "seen the wolf," you have glimpsed something that frightened you. This was originally associated with people who had temporarily lost their voice, based on the old superstition that a wolf could strike one dumb.

During the Middle Ages it was believed that wolves' eyes shone at night like lamps lit by the devil.

The following story was often told about Saint Francis and the wolf at Gubbino. In medieval times wolves would often come down from the mountains during famines and steal food and kill people. This was the case in the small French town of Gubbino. The townspeople were terrified until finally one day Saint Francis and his disciples went out to meet the wolf. When the wolf ran toward him with fangs bared, Saint Francis met him and demanded that he neither harm him nor anyone else. In return, Saint Francis promised that the townspeople would feed the wolf. Legend says that the wolf agreed and for two years lived in the town and was known as *Fra Lupo,* or brother wolf.

In Egyptian mythology, the god Upuaat was sometimes depicted as a wolf whose job it was to help souls past various gates that led to the spirit world.

GRAY WOLF

COMMON NAME: Wolverine

SCIENTIFIC NAME: *Gulo gulo*

DESCRIPTION: The wolverine resembles a small bear. The head is broad and powerful, and the animal is round and close to the ground. The head and body measure 28 to 34 inches; the tail adds another 8 to 9 inches. It is an exceptionally strong animal, with dark brown or reddish brown fur and pale yellow bands across the face.

HABITAT AND RANGE: Wolverines live in timbered areas in northern latitudes around the world.

A Blackfoot hero legend tells of a Scar-face, a poor young man who wishes to marry a beautiful girl. She has refused marriage proposals from all the rich men of the tribe, but she considers this man's proposal in spite of the scar across his cheek.

The young woman instructs Scarface to go to the sun to receive his blessing for the marriage. The young man agrees, but, while looking for the path to the sun, he gets lost. He asks the wolf for directions, but the wolf says to ask the bear, and the bear says he should ask the wolverine.

Scarface cannot find the wolverine and sits down, hungry and discouraged, and cries to the wolverine for help. The wolverine appears behind him and asks what he wants. The man explains that he has become lost on the way to Sun to ask for a marriage blessing. The wolverine takes pity on him and tells him that he will show him the path first thing in the morning. When the sun peeks through the mountains, the wolverine keeps its promise, and the man finds the sun, receives the blessing, and marries the girl.

The eastern Algonquian Indians considered wolverines trickster animals. For many tribes this animal symbolized strength and persistence. According to one North American Indian legend, Wolverine helped Fisher repair a hole in the sky.

Wolverine has become a universal symbol of greed and gluttony. In fact, common names for the wolverine include skunk bear and glutton.

WOLVERINE

INSECTS
AND
ARACHNIDS

COMMON NAME: Ant, Carpenter

SCIENTIFIC NAME: *Camponotus ferrugineus*

DESCRIPTION: Coloration of this ant may be reddish brown or black. The abdomen is joined to the thorax with a narrow point. Antennae, composed of twelve segments, are bent and do not have a club.

HABITAT AND RANGE: A wood-nesting species, carpenter ants dig nests out of fallen trees and stumps. These ants also dig in decayed wood in houses and should be controlled, although they are rarely as destructive as termites. They are found throughout North America, west to Texas.

The *Book of Beasts* relates the following Central American folktale: When a man was suddenly blessed with the ability to understand the language of ants, he asked, "What is God like? Does he resemble an ant?" The ant replied, "God? Resemble an ant? Of course not! We only have one sting, God has two!"

Many folk sayings include reference to ants. The Japanese say that "An ant hole may collapse an embankment." A Malaysian saying is "Where does the ant die except in sugar?" A saying from Persia claims that "In the ant's house the dew is a flood."

Ants were thought to predict the weather. An open ant hill was thought to mean clear weather, while a closed one indicated an approaching storm. Also, according to an American Indian superstition, when you saw ants marching in a straight line, it was thought to mean rain, a superstition that has little credibility since many species of ants most often travel in straight lines. It was also thought that when ants are busy, bad weather is on the way.

In Hindu mythology ants symbolize the small and petty things of life. In contrast to this, Hindus also believe that ants are superior to humans. On certain holy days they actually feed ants because they believe ants are associated with the dead.

Often in mythology, similar stories are told in unrelated cultures, and such is the case with tales of the ants. The Hopi believed the first people were ants. This is similar to the Greek myth of the ant-men, in which Hera becomes jealous of her husband, Zeus, and a young maiden named Aegina. In revenge, she sends a plague to the country from which the girl came.

The plague kills thousands of people until the king fears his country will never be populated again. In desperation, he asks Zeus for help, and Zeus turns the ants into men, who were called the Myrmidons and whose leader was Achilles.

The Japanese hold ants in high esteem, as evidenced by the characters that make up the Japanese word for ant. The first is the character for insect, and the others are the characters for unselfishness, courtesy, and justice.

In Arabian countries it was customary for the father to put an ant in the hands of a new-

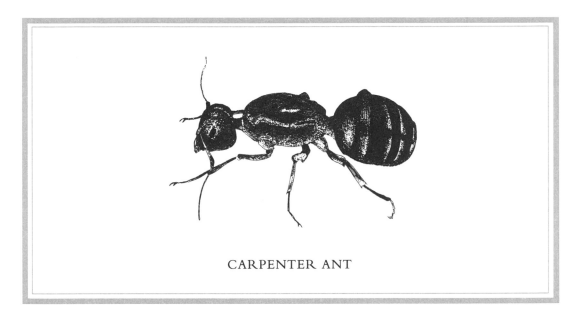

CARPENTER ANT

born son and say, "May this boy turn out clever and skillful." West Africans believe that the ant serves as messenger for the serpent god. Hebrew people consider the ant wise, and in Hinduism black ants are sacred. In France bad luck will follow you if you destroy an ant's nest.

In the southwestern United States, the Pueblo Indians believe that ants are vindictive and cause disease. These illnesses can only be cured by specific "ant doctors." In Taos, Indian women believed they would turn into red ants if they slept with white men.

The medicinal use of ants is legendary. Particularly in countries where large ants are found, these insects were sometimes used to close flesh wounds and incisions. The carpenter ant was most often used for this purpose, and references in Hindu writing indicate that this practice was common as early as 1000 B.C. The ants were put beside the wound and allowed to bite the surrounding flesh. Once the jaws were in place, the bodies were pinched off, leaving the head behind to keep the wound closed.

Ants were used for healing in other ways.

A Russian cure for rheumatism was to pour boiling water over an anthill. Oil extracted from the Formica ant was used to cure gout and palsy. Maine lumberjacks ate black ants to prevent scurvy. In the Ozarks these same large black ants were ground into a salve mixed with oil and rubbed on babies' legs in the hope the child would learn to walk quickly.

Tea made from white ants was used by Black Americans to cure whooping cough, and in Morocco ants were fed to patients suffering from lethargy.

The Arawak Indians believe that if you are bitten on the foot by an ant, something good will happen to you. Before members of this tribe are allowed to marry, they must undergo the "ordeal of the ants," in which they are placed under a tent full of these biting insects.

A favorite country saying is "What would the ant do if she but had the head of a bull?" It is also said that "an ant may work its heart out, but cannot make honey." In the vein of "Silence is golden" is this saying: "None preaches better than the ant and she says nothing."

For more ant folklore, see "Grasshopper," page 124.

COMMON NAME: Bee, Honey

SCIENTIFIC NAME: *Apis mellifera*

DESCRIPTION: The queen is largest of the honeybees, measuring almost $3/4$ inch across her abdomen. Male drones are $5/8$ inch long, female workers $3/8$ to $5/8$ inch. All honeybees are slightly reddish brown with black rings on the abdomen. The wings are clear.

HABITAT AND RANGE: This species is found in North America and Europe. Similar honeybee species are found in Asia. Though *A. mellifer* is completely domesticated and lives in hives provided by humans, sometimes a swarm will leave to form a wild colony.

Settlers brought honeybees to the United States in the seventeenth century as a source of sweetener for baking and cooking. Although sugar has been known for only 200 years, honey has been known since prehistoric times. According to Greek mythology, Zeus was raised on milk and honey, and in the stories from the Bible the Hebrews were tempted by a land flowing with milk and honey. Karma, the Hindu god of love, had a bowstring made of bees. With the widespread use of sugar and artificial sweeteners, honey is no longer an important economic commodity, and today the honeybee is more valuable for its pollinating capabilities than for its honey and wax.

In ancient times beeswax had many uses. Egyptians used it to cover writing tablets so letters could be rubbed out and used again. Greeks used it in painting and sculpture.

In many different mythologies, honey was believed to be capable of restoring life. Zeus was sometimes called Melissaios, or "bee man," based on the legend that he had a son, conceived through his illicit union with a wood nymph, whom he hid in the woods to protect from the wrath of his wife, Hera. He sent the boy food by way of the bees.

Aesop tells the story that a queen bee went to Mount Olympus one day and offered honey to Zeus, who was delighted with the gift and promised to give the queen bee anything she wanted. The queen bee then asked for a sting that killed anyone who tried to take the honey. Zeus was not happy with this but granted the queen bee her request, adding that every time a bee stings a man, the bee will die.

This latter statement is not only myth but fact as well. The stinging mechanism in honeybees is composed of sharp barbs. When the stinger penetrates flesh, the bee cannot extract it without pulling out part of his abdomen, an act that instantly kills the insect. Hornets, wasps, and bumblebees do not have these barbs on their stingers and are capable of stinging repeatedly.

There are several stories about the origin of the bee. Christians say they were created by God to supply wax for the candles of the

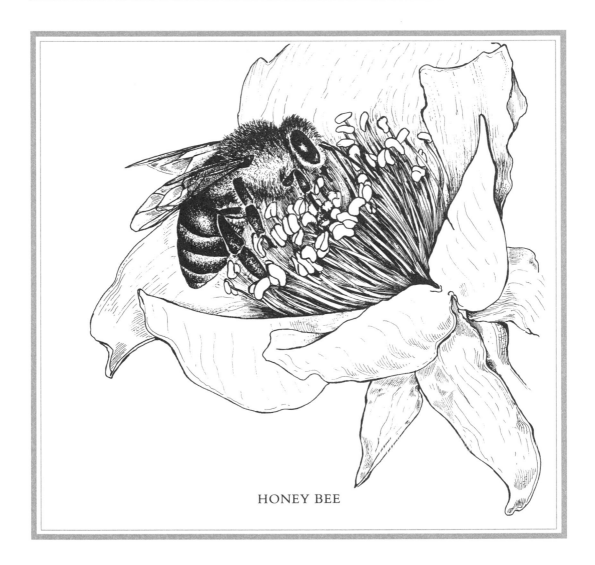

HONEY BEE

church. In Egypt it was believed that Ra, the sun god, made bees from his tears. The Roman poet Virgil contended, however, that bees first came from the carcasses of dead oxen. The queen bee (originally thought to be the king bee) came from oxens' brains, and the worker bees were produced from the flesh. Early Oriental writings also refer to the "ox-born bee."

During wars, swarms of bees were let loose on enemy armies, an early practice of biological warfare. Reports of this practice are available as recently as the Thirty Year's War between 1618–1648.

Superstitions about bees and death are common in many cultures. It was believed that one must tell the bees when a family member dies, otherwise the bees will desert their hive.

A bee flying to a sleeping child is a sign of good fortune. If a bee flies into a room, it is an omen of good news or of a stranger coming. If a bee lights on your head and stays there, you will rise to great heights. If you see a swarm of bees and make a wish, the wish will come true.

In reference to the weather, if bees stay in the hive for a long time, rain is coming. A swarm of bees in May is worth a load of hay, but a swarm in July is not worth a fly.

An African saying suggests that the earth is a beehive, and we all enter by the same door. The French say that what is not good for the swarm is not good for the bee, and the best honey isn't obtained by squeezing.

An old proverb says that the bee sucks honey out of the bitterest flowers. Another says that bees that have honey in their mouth have stings in their tail. Still another says, "No honey, no work, no money."

"His head is full of bees" is a Scottish saying that refers to a drunkard. This is very different from "having a bee in your bonnet," which means an idea you just can't let go of. Remember that "one bee is better than a handful of flies," but also keep in mind that "luxury has honey in her mouth, gall in her heart, and sting in her tail."

A folktale from Siberia tells how the bee

got its bumble. Long ago there was a seven-headed giant named Delbegen. One day he called the bee to him and ordered it to take a bite from each creature and come back to tell him which was the sweetest.

The bee flew off and began his task. He took a bite out of rabbit and deer and dog and cat and every other animal, and then took a bite out of a man and immediately began to sing, "Man is sweetest! Man is sweetest!" At this the man became frightened that Delbegen would eat him, so he caught the bee and took out its tongue so it could not report back to the giant.

When the little bee returned to Delbegen, he tried to say "Man is sweetest," but without a tongue it sounded like "bzzz, bzzz," which is what the bee says even today.

Saint Anthony of Padua, who lived from A.D. 340–397, adopted the beehive as his symbol. According to legend, when this saint was an infant, a swarm of bees landed on his mouth but did not harm him. This was taken as a symbol of great fortune.

COMMON NAME: Beetle, Scarab
SCIENTIFIC NAME: *Phyllophaga fervida*

DESCRIPTION: Scarab beetles vary in length from $^1/_{10}$ inch to 5 inches long. Though most often black or dark, this beetle can also show bright iridescent colors. The end sections of the antennae can spread like a fan.

HABITAT AND RANGE: Found throughout the United States, southern Canada, and northern Mexico in a wide variety of habitats.

SCARAB BEETLE

The name beetle is from the Anglo-Saxon word, *bitan*, meaning "to bite." This beetle is also called a June bug.

A Pueblo Indian story tells that the beetle was given a sackful of stars to take from the underworld to the world above. Lazy beetle became tired when the sack got heavy, so he bit a hole in the bottom of the sack and the stars flew out all over the heavens. The Cochiti Indians tell a similar story in which the beetle is so ashamed of his laziness that even today he hides his face in the dirt when approached.

In the British Isles it was considered bad luck to kill a beetle. To kill a beetle was also thought to bring rain, thunder, and lightning. To see a black beetle anywhere in the house was thought to mean bad luck, and if it crawled across one's shoe, it was a sign of impending death. If a beetle falls on its back, you will have good luck if you turn it over.

In ancient Egypt the beetle was of enormous significance. The small dung beetle was thought to be a symbol of eternal life. The likeness of this beetle was carved into stones or jewels and was made into scarabs or amulets that were worn, used in burial ceremonies, or given as gifts. To wear a scarab carved from an emerald was said to make one's eyesight more piercing.

One of the most unusual characteristics of this beetle is that it rolls dung into a ball and pushes the ball ahead of itself as it moves. Thus this small beetle became symbolic of the sun moving across the sky and also of self-created power. It was associated with Khepera, Egyptian god of creation and immortality. (In actuality, the ball of dung serves as a receptacle for the beetle's eggs. When the larvae hatch, they have an immediate food source.)

When an Egyptian died, his heart was removed and was replaced with a scarab. This served to excuse the soul from any sins that might have been committed during his lifetime. The scarab was believed to be the means by which the soul triumphed in the afterlife.

Scarab beetles, which appeared in spring with the rainy season and the consequent rising of the Nile River, were closely associated with the fertility and abundance of life made possible by the Nile.

To the Bedouins of Egypt, eating the dung beetle was an important part of the initiation ceremonies of young boys reaching adolescence. Dung beetles were also sometimes used as medicine. Pliny wrote that it was useful to carry the beetle, wrapped in linen and tied with a red string, as protection against "quartan ague," which is believed to be a form of malaria.

According to folk wisdom, "The beetle is a thing of beauty in its mother's eye."

COMMON NAME: Butterfly, Black Swallowtail
SCIENTIFIC NAME: *Papilio polyxenes*

DESCRIPTION: This large butterfly has a wingspan of 2 3/4 to 6 inches. Wings are black with yellow spots along their margins. Blue spots are found on the lower wings.

HABITAT AND RANGE: Found throughout the United States and into Mexico in many different habitats from deserts, forests, and grasslands to gardens and suburban areas.

The Papago Indians tell this story of how the butterflies came to be: Soon after the Earth-Maker created the earth, Iitoi, Elder Brother, was walking in the sunshine and heard children's voices as they played happily. Moved by this happy scene, he decided to make something. Into his magic bag he put the colors from flowers and fallen leaves, and yellow pollen, white cornmeal, green pine needles, and a bit of golden sunlight. Then he called the children together and told them to open the bag. When they did, the first butterflies flew out, and the children's hearts were glad.

The name butterfly came from the butter-yellow color common on the wings of many species. In Germany the name is *butterfliege*, in Danish *botrvlieg*.

In some parts of the world, butterflies are regarded as gods, in other parts, as witches.

BLACK SWALLOWTAIL BUTTERFLY

According to folklore in Europe and Japan and from native tribes of North America and the Pacific Islands, the butterfly is the soul of man. The Maori believe that a person's soul returns to earth after death in the form of a butterfly. The Finno-Gric people believe the soul leaves the body as a butterfly while the person is asleep and this accounts for dreams.

To the Greeks, the soul was a tiny person with butterfly wings. In southern Germany it was believed that the dead are reborn as children who fly about as butterflies. This is why many medieval angels have butterfly wings rather than bird wings.

In the Solomon Islands, the belief was held that the dead can choose the form in which they will return to earth. Many choose to come back as butterflies. When a butterfly dies it is thought to be the end of the soul forever.

In Burma, rice is said to have a butterfly soul. A trail of husks and unthreshed rice is carefully laid from the field to the granary so that the soul may find the grain. Otherwise, none will grow the following year.

In many cultures, the butterfly is worshipped as god and creator. One Sumatran tribe says they are descended from three brothers hatched from eggs laid by a butterfly. A North American Indian myth says the creator, Chiowotmahki, took the form of a butterfly and flew over the world until he found a suitable place for man to live.

In Mexico the butterfly is a symbol of the fertility of the earth. Samoans believed if they caught a butterfly, it would strike them dead.

In many parts of Europe butterflies are considered taboo, and in Scotland, Friesland, and Bosnia, they are considered witches. Serbians look on the butterfly as the soul of a witch and believe that if they can find the witch's body and turn it around while she sleeps, the butterfly-soul will not be able to find her mouth and reenter, and the witch will die. In Bulgaria dark butterflies indicate that sickness is coming, and in Brunswick if the first butterfly of the season is white, it is an omen of death. If it is yellow, a birth is pending, and if variegated, a marriage will happen soon. Butterflies were also thought to be disguised fairies who steal butter and milk, and it is thought to be unlucky to capture them.

Like other insects, butterflies were also used to predict weather. If the first butterfly seen in spring is white, it is supposed to indicate a rainy summer. If dark, the summer would be full of thunderstorms, and if yellow, sunny weather will prevail during the coming months.

Benjamin Franklin said, "What is a butterfly? At best, he's but a caterpillar dressed."

Caterpillars, immature forms of the butterfly, were thought to be created from Devil's tears. The German name, *Teufelskatze*, means "Devil's cat." In Switzerland and elsewhere, tree spirits were considered responsible for the caterpillar. The trees were said to have sent caterpillars to the fields to annoy folks.

The oil from a cabbage caterpillar was mixed with oil for rubbing on a wound resulting from the bite of a poisonous snake. In England, carrying a caterpillar was thought to end a fever and was also used for help with a toothache.

Butterflies dancing through falling snow!
What a wonderful sight it would be!"

—*Demaru*

COMMON NAME: Centipede

SCIENTIFIC NAME: *Scutigera coleoptrata*

DESCRIPTION: In spite of the name, the actual number of legs varies from 15 to 173. The common household centipede has thin, spidery legs and long antennae.

HABITAT AND RANGE: Centipedes are common throughout the eastern half of the United States in varied land habitats including around houses, under bark, and among rocks and leaf litter.

In China the immortal or shape-shifting centipede is one of the protagonists in a battle between shape-shifters. During combat, one of the warriors changes into a centipede surrounded by a black cloud that emits fog, allowing him to escape to safety.

Along with the scorpion, snake, lizard, and toad, the centipede is considered one of the five venoms in China and is sometimes painted on ceremonial cakes on the Double Fifth—the fifth day of the fifth moon of the year. A mixture of wine and phosphorus

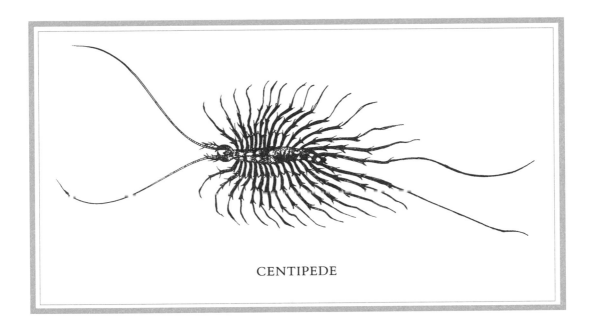

CENTIPEDE

rubbed on heads of infants on this day will protect them against the five venoms. In India, legend says that the king, who was said to have suffered from a centipede in the head, found relief by rubbing his head with this same concoction.

The word centipede was taboo in Java and among Malayan tin miners. In Tahiti two centipedes were thought to be shadows of the medicine gods and were never disturbed or killed.

Folk superstition contends that if a centipede can be made to crawl over a sick person, they will get well.

A poem by Mrs. Howard Craster stated that:

> *The centipede was happy quite until a toad*
> *   in fun*
> *Said, "Pray, which leg goes after which?"*
> *That worked her mind to such a pitch,*
> *She lay distracted in a ditch,*
> *Considering how to run.*

COMMON NAME: Cicada, Dog Day
SCIENTIFIC NAME: *Tibicen canicularis*

DESCRIPTION: These insects measure 1 1/4 to 1 1/2 inches long and have transparent wings intersected with dark brown or bluish veins. Antennae on females are short; on males they are long and slender. Adults emerge in late summer and live through early fall. The characteristic buzzing sound is particularly noticeable during hot August days.

HABITAT AND RANGE: This species is found throughout the United States. Eggs are deposited on small branches of shrubs or trees. Nymphs live underneath the ground for 2 years, feeding on roots.

Many ancient cultures believed that catastrophic events occurred if people offended the gods by breaking certain taboos. In the Andaman Islands there is a species of cicada that sings early in the morning and again in the evening. The people were prohibited from killing this small insect and from making noise during its morning or evening song.

An ancient myth suggested that when the world was first created, people (called the Ancestors) were the only animals. One evening the Ancestors made a noise while the cicadas sang, and the gods were so incensed they created a cyclone that turned the Ancestors into birds, fish, and jungle animals.

Another myth suggests the importance of the cicada to the Andamanese. In the beginning of the world it was always day. One day Sir Monitor Lizard (a mythical lizard who had dominion over land and sea, see Lizard page 154) found a cicada and rubbed it between its feet. The cicada cried out, and the lizard crushed it. Immediately darkness fell, and the Ancestors could not get the day back. It was not until Sir Ant sang that day returned and since then, darkness and light have alternated.

The life cycle of the cicada led the Oraibian Indians to believe that this insect represented resurrection. The cicada, which splits its shell, emerges as a new white insect, and then leaves behind an empty shell, all indicated that the cicada held the power to create new life. Because of this symbolism, the cicada was thought to be powerful medicine; a salve was made from the insects' bodies and was used on soldiers who had suffered terrible wounds on the battlefield.

Although beetle amulets were by far the most common amulets in Egypt, cicada amulets were also made and put on the tongues of people who died. Usually carved from brown jade, a cicada amulet was thought to be the highest possible honor to bestow on a deceased friend.

Cicadas were used as food among the southern Siamese. The people attracted them by sitting around a fire in the late evening,

DOG DAY CICADA

clapping their hands in unison. The female cicadas were attracted by the sound (or the vibrations) and arrived in swarms.

The Cherokee call the cicadas "jarflies," and the common saying, "The jarfly has brought the beans," originated because the cicadas begin to sing in midsummer just as the first crops of beans come in. In the American South, it was believed that if you heard the cicadas sing at night, the next day would be hot.

The Chinese kept male cicadas in cages for their "song," which is actually more of a whistle than a song. A Chinese poet described the sound in this way: *"A single note, wandering in strange keys, An air yet fraught with undertone of hidden harmony."*

The Greeks tell a story about two talented musicians, Eunomis and Aristo, who participated in a contest to determine who was the best player. Aristo played brilliantly and with technical mastery. Eunomis played with great feeling and understanding of the music, but toward the end of his last piece his C string broke. Eunomis kept playing, and at just the right moment a cicada flew down and sang his one note and Eunomis won the contest. Since that time the Greeks have considered the cicada the symbol for melody.

COMMON NAME: Cockroach, Oriental
SCIENTIFIC NAME: *Blatta orientalis*

DESCRIPTION: Cockroaches have a flattened, oval body, brown or black in color. The legs have distinct hairs. The antennae are long and slender, and the wings are small.

HABITAT AND RANGE: Widely distributed, this species was introduced from Asia. These insects are most active at night and feed on food crumbs and a variety of other items. They are more prominent in the South than in northern areas.

Folktales say that the cockroach originated in Finland, though fossil records indicate that it is indigenous to all parts of the world.

In Russia and France the cockroach is thought to be a protecting spirit, and its presence in the house is considered lucky. If the roach leaves, it is thought to be a sign of bad luck. In the United States, it is thought that sweeping them out on Good Friday or impaling one on a pin will scare off all the rest.

In Ireland it was thought that witches sometimes take the shape of cockroaches to plague farmers.

Jamaican stories often include cockroaches. The Antiguan story "Why Fowl Catch Cockroaches" tells how Cockroach, who is always playing and singing, meets a tragic end.

In folk medicine the cockroach is used in the treatment of urinary disorders, for worms in children, for epilepsy, and for other ills.

Blacks in Mississippi put a large jar in the hearth ashes overnight. If there is a cockroach in it the next morning, they believe they have caught a witch. Whatever fate befalls the cockroach will also befall the witch.

Proverbs referring to the cockroach include "The cockroach is always wrong when arguing with the chicken" and "Cockroaches never get justice when a chicken is the judge."

"Sound as a roach" refers to Saint Roche, the patron saint for all those afflicted with the plague. People offered prayers to this saint in the hopes that he could make them as sound as himself.

An old folk belief was that a cockroach would eat at your toenails at night unless your feet were well covered by the bedclothes. It was also believed that if a roach flew against you, death would soon follow.

ORIENTAL COCKROACH

COMMON NAME: Cricket, House

SCIENTIFIC NAME: *Acheta domesticus*

DESCRIPTION: Crickets measure $1/2$ to 1 inch long. The house cricket, introduced from Europe, has a light-colored head with dark crossbands. The antennae are very long, and the back legs are large and prominent.

HABITAT AND RANGE: Found in the eastern two-thirds of the United States, it is quite common in gardens, fields, and suburban areas.

The name cricket is from a German word meaning "little creaker," referring to the insect's chirping song.

In China it was believed that a house with a cricket in it will enjoy much happiness. This belief was so widely held that many Chinese families kept crickets as pets. Even today you can buy small brass "cricket boxes" styled from the Chinese boxes used to hold live crickets.

This Oriental belief was taken to Europe with the first traders, and now in many parts of Europe and the United States crickets are thought to bring good luck. It is considered bad luck to kill one. In some areas it is believed that if one cricket is killed, his family will come and eat your clothes. It was also considered dangerous to imitate the chirp of the cricket.

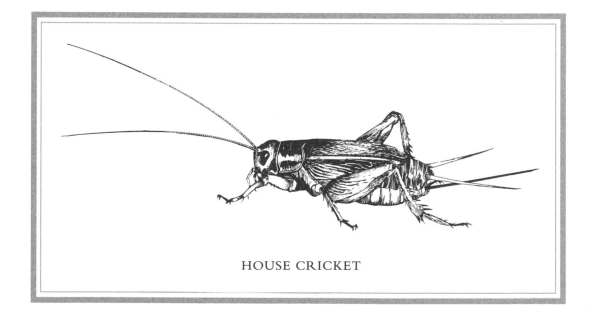

HOUSE CRICKET

If a cricket is seen in the chimney and then subsequently leaves the house, it is considered a sign that death will soon visit the house.

In Ireland a cricket heard chirping on Christmas Eve is called the king of all luck.

Pliny the Elder suggested that twenty crickets brewed in red wine were a good cure for asthma. A decoction of crickets was also thought to be good for earaches.

The Cherokee drank tea made from crickets in order to sing as beautifully as the cricket.

As predictor, the cricket forecasts rain, death, and the approach of an absent lover. A country formula for determining the temperature is to divide the number of cricket chirps per minute by four, add forty, and the answer is the temperature in degrees Fahrenheit.

If a cricket was heard in the house, it was thought that rain was on the way. In the American Ozarks, to hear a cricket in the house meant good fortune and prosperity.

Known as the "barber" by some native tribes, the cricket has special structures called a file and a scraper on its wings, which make noise during warm weather.

COMMON NAME: Dragonfly, Green Darner

SCIENTIFIC NAME: *Anax junius*

DESCRIPTION The length of the body is 2³/₄ to 3¹/₈ inches; the wingspan is 4³/₈ inches. Wings are held horizontally to the body, and cannot be folded in close to the body even when the insect is at rest. The thorax is greenish, the abdomen bluish gray. Translucent wings darken as the insect ages.

HABITAT AND RANGE: These insects are found near still water (ponds, lakes, and slow moving streams) throughout North America.

The face of the dragonfly
Is practically nothing
But eyes.
—Chisoku

According to a myth retold in Tony Hillerman's charming *The Boy Who Made Dragonfly*, the Zuni people at one time experienced a drought so terrible that the tribe was forced to leave their village and beg for charity from a neighboring tribe. The people knew the journey would be long and difficult and when it was discovered that a boy and his sister had been mistakenly left behind, the elders did not go back after them, believing it was kinder to let them sleep and die from hunger than to subject them to the dangers of the journey.

The young boy loved his sister and tried to cheer her up by making her a wonderful toy out of cornstalks. Although he had tried to make a butterfly, the wings were too narrow, the eyes were not quite right, and the

GREEN DARNER DRAGONFLY

creature he produced was unlike anything they had ever seen before. The children called him Dragonfly. One day this cornstalk creature went to the council of the gods and asked for food for the children. The gods were impressed with the way the boy loved and cared for his sister. They sent corn for them to eat and gave them wisdom, and when they were grown made them leaders of their people.

The Oglala Sioux believed that the dragonfly had the ability to avoid being hurt by man or beast and would never be injured by lightning. This power was desired by all people, and the dragonfly was thus held in high esteem.

The dragonfly is sometimes called "Mosquito Hawk" because it catches food by creating a basket from its six legs and scooping up its prey while flying.

In Japan, the dragonfly is considered a symbol for victory.

In many parts of the world, the dragonfly is thought to be a "snake doctor" in that it was protection against or cure for snake bite. It was very bad to kill a dragonfly because it was thought that the snake would then come to harm you in revenge.

Around the Isle of Wright it was believed that the dragonfly would hover around good boys who went fishing but would sting the bad boys who were fishing.

In rural parts of the United States, it was thought that dragonflies would sew up various anatomical openings—lips, eyelids, or ears—and was thus sometimes called "devil's darning needle."

COMMON NAME: Firefly

SCIENTIFIC NAME: *Photuris pyralis*

DESCRIPTION: A small beetle only ¼ to ⅞ inch long, fireflies are most easily identified at night when their tails flash with a bright light. The bodies are soft, and the head is small and round. The thorax has yellow markings. The light organs are larger in the males.

HABITAT AND RANGE: Common throughout the eastern United States in open grasslands.

Fireflies are magical creatures, beloved by many different cultures. Ojibway Indian children chanted the following before going to bed:

Fluttering white-fire insects.
Wavering small-fire beasts!
Wave little stars about my bed!
Weave little stars into my sleep!

Henry Wadsworth Longfellow, in his poem "The Song of Hiawatha," wrote:

At the door on summer evenings,
Sat the little Hiawatha;
. . . Saw the fire-fly, Wah-wah-taysee,
Flitting through the dusk of evening,
With the twinkle of its candle,
Lighting up the brakes and bushes . . .

In China and Japan there are many stories and legends about the firefly. One story says that a young man, Ch'e Yin, desired nothing more than to learn. Although he had no money to buy oil for his lamp, he collected fireflies so that he could continue to study long after sundown. *Keisetsu,* a Japanese word translated as "fireflies and snow" and meaning hard work and diligence, is derived from the legend of Ch'e Yin. Conscientious Japanese students were thought to have studied by the light of fireflies or the light reflected off snow after the sun set.

The related elater beetles in the West Indies are luminous and were used instead of jewels by ladies going to fancy parties. They would collect the fireflies and fasten them on their dresses and in their hair with pins, and even sometimes put them on the trappings of their horses. It was said that if the beetles were to be used more than once, the ladies would feed them cane sugar to keep them alive.

A sad Chinese legend tells of a wicked woman who often beat her stepson. One day she gave the boy some money to go buy oil from a neighboring village. Along the way the boy lost the money, and terrified of returning to his stepmother empty-handed, he searched and searched for the money until it was quite dark and he fell into the river and drowned. Even in death, however, the boy feared his evil stepmother, and the legend says that every summer night you can see the boy holding a light and looking for the lost money. The light is the little firefly.

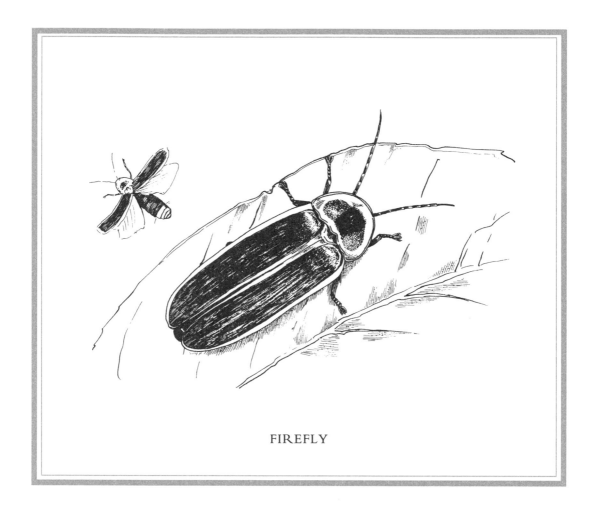

FIREFLY

Fireflies are sometimes thought to be stars that have left heaven to wander the earth. In Japan, it is thought that fireflies were the souls of warriors who died for their country.

The light of the firefly is cool light, without heat, a fact that has led to some unusual superstitions and symbolism. In Buddhism, fireflies represent shallow knowledge, which does little to shed light on ignorance.

In Bengal it was believed that swallowing a firefly would cure night blindness. In parts of the United States, it was thought that if a firefly flew into your eye, it would put your eye out.

In Ontario, it was thought that if you killed a firefly, you would be struck by lightning the next day.

The Penobscot Indians believed fireflies were harbingers of salmon. In the American South, a firefly in the house meant good luck.

COMMON NAME: Flea, Cat

SCIENTIFIC NAME: *Ctenocephalides felis*

DESCRIPTION: A tiny, wingless creature, the cat flea has a flattened body with a tough outer covering that makes it difficult to kill. The head gently curves from front to back.

HABITAT AND RANGE: Found worldwide on live cats.

Tiny and irritating, fleas have been pestering humans, felines, canines, and other animals for thousands of years. As John Donne put it so succinctly, "The flea though he kill none, he does all the harm he can."

Because the flea is both tiny and exceedingly irritating, much folklore is concerned with this insect. According to Danish legend, the flea was sent to pester mankind as punishment for being so lazy. A Flemish counterpart to this story suggests that a flea was created to give women work. Folk sayings about the flea abound. Thomas Fuller suggests that one "Do nothing hastily but the catching of fleas."

Although "a reasonable amount of fleas is good for dog, for it keeps him from brooding," you should also remember that "he who lies with dogs shall rise up with fleas," and "the fatter the flea, the leaner the dog."

Fleas have never been known to be timid,

CAT FLEA

as indicated by the saying, "That's a valiant flea that dare eat his breakfast on the lip of a lion." In Germany and Austria it was believed that if you are bitten on the hand by a flea, you are about to be kissed. In many countries it is believed that fleas will leave the body of one who is about to die.

Getting rid of fleas has been a challenge for many centuries, and many folk customs address this problem. Pliny says that on hearing the first cuckoo of spring, if you gather up the dirt under your right foot and sprinkle this around the house, you will not be troubled with fleas throughout the year.

In England it is believed that fleas return on the first of March and if you are able to keep the house closed securely during that day, the fleas won't come in. If you miss this opportunity, you can always jump over the Midsummer's Eve fire to rid yourself of fleas.

In the United States, a house could be rid of fleas by driving them away with a splinter of wood from a tree struck by lightning. The Irish perform a similar ritual using a piece of spearmint or foxglove.

In 1733 Jonathan Swift wrote in his Poems II, "Big fleas have little fleas up their backs to bite them, and little fleas have lesser fleas, and so ad infinitum."

When you are in a hurry, remember that "nothing should be done in haste except gripping a flea."

COMMON NAME: Fly, House

SCIENTIFIC NAME: *Musca domestica*

DESCRIPTION: The common house fly measures ¹/₈ to ¹/₄ inch long. It is gray with four black stripes on the thorax. Its eyes are reddish, its wings are clear, and its legs are hairy.

HABITAT AND RANGE: Found near food, garbage, or animal manure throughout the world except in Antarctica.

The Roman god Baal was called Lord of the Flies, and his idol was usually portrayed in the image of a giant fly. Baal was thought to hold the power to protect people from flies.

A North American Indian myth tells why flies are scavengers. Once there were two tribes of people who lived close to one another. One tribe was industrious and worked all summer long to put away food for the winter.

The other tribe played and wasted time during the summer and had no food when the cold came, but the first tribe took pity on them and shared its food.

The next year the lazy tribe again played during the months of growth and harvest, and when fall came again they had no food. The hard-working tribe was tired of doing all the work for both tribes and decided to move away. The lazy tribe moaned and wailed

HOUSE FLY

about their fate until the Great Spirit decided to teach them a lesson. He gave the hardworking tribe wings and made them bees, and to the lazy tribe He said, "You too will have wings, but while the bees go from flower to flower to eat the yellow honey, your food will be whatever people happen to throw away, and you will be known as flies."

The Mission Indians in California tell this tale of why flies rub their two front legs together: The Maker, Tee-chai-pai, saw that his people did not have enough food to last forever. He gave them three choices: they could die and be through with life forever, they could die and come back, or they could live forever. The people could not make a choice and bickered back and forth until a fly heard them and in disgust at their bickering said, "Just die and be done with it." The people did as he suggested and ever since that time the fly has rubbed its feet together, begging forgiveness from the people for the words uttered so hastily.

In Lapland, shamans would go into a trance to better serve their tribes. During this time, it was believed that the shaman's spirit had left his body and so the "empty" body was carefully protected even from flies. If a fly touched the body at this vulnerable time, it was believed that the spirit would not return to the body.

A proverb suggests that "the fly that plays too long in the candle, singes his wings at last." A French saying suggests that you "don't imitate the fly before you have wings."

COMMON NAME: Grasshopper, Carolina

SCIENTIFIC NAME: *Dissosteira carolina*

DESCRIPTION: Dull brown, this grasshopper measures $1/2$ to 2 inches in length as an adult. The body is elongated, with long wings that remain close to the body when the insect is at rest. The antennae are short; the hind legs very long.

HABITAT AND RANGE: Carolina grasshopper inhabits grasslands and fields from the eastern coast of the United States to as far west as the Rocky Mountains, south to Texas and Georgia, and north to southern Maine.

One of the most famous poems about insects is one about the grasshopper and the ant by La Fontaine (probably originally a fable from Aesop). The grasshopper spent her days singing in the fields and did not work at all to store food for the winter. When cold weather came and the sweet grass was gone from the field, Grasshopper went to see her friend, Ant, who had worked diligently all summer preparing for these cold days.

When Grasshopper asked for food, Ant said, why didn't you work in the summer? Grasshopper answered that she had been busy singing. Ant replied, "Then dance the wintertime away."

This respect for diligence is also reflected in the Bible's Book of Proverbs (6:6), which admonishes men to "follow the ways of the ant and become wise." This ancient fable may also be the origin of the proverb, "Hold on, wait for the grasshopper," meaning to hang in there until better times come along.

A southwestern American Indian legend says that grasshoppers brought bread to the earth and it happened in this way: All the shamans from all the tribes gathered to see which of them was the most powerful. They bickered about who made the sun until the sun finally disappeared. None of the shamans could bring it back, so the animals tried. Grasshopper tried first, but instead of bringing back the sun, he brought bread. Deer tried as well, and brought Yucca fruit, and the chipmunk brought strawberries.

The Ojibway Indians tell this tale of the origin of the grasshopper: Long ago when Manabush was young, he was walking through the mountains when he suddenly smelled delicious smoke. It seemed to be coming from a cave high up in the mountains. On entering the cave, he found a giant smoking a pipe.

Manabush liked the smell of the tobacco and told the giant, "The Indians do not have this, I will make it a gift to them." The giant said there was no more tobacco but Manabush saw many bear hides full of tobacco in the cave. He grabbed one of these bags and ran out of the cave and through the mountains, with the giant running and jumping

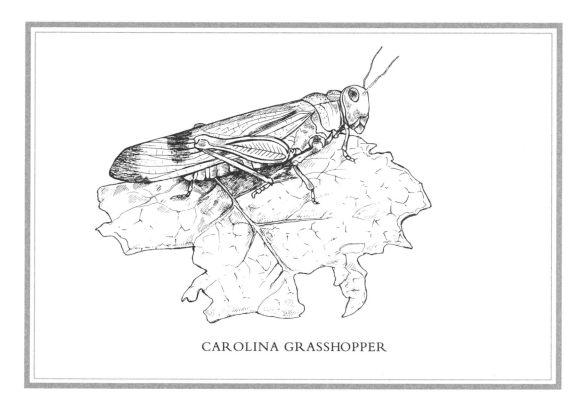

CAROLINA GRASSHOPPER

behind him. Finally the giant caught up with Manabush, who turned and told him he was greedy and selfish. Manabush spoke a magic word, turning the giant into a grasshopper who would spend the rest of his days jumping from one place to another, living in the tobacco fields but never enjoying the tobacco.

In the symbolism of ancient Greece, the grasshopper represented the aristocracy, a custom adopted in the heraldry of Europe.

In China it was believed that the spirit of the grasshopper served to protect against destructive insects and was thought to bring good luck and the promise of many sons.

An old folk superstition said that if you catch a grasshopper and bite his head off, you'll find money.

"Knee high to a grasshopper" was a favorite phrase indicating the height of small children. "It is useless to stretch the grasshopper's leg," meant that it was a waste of time trying to do things that just won't work.

COMMON NAME: Katydid, True

SCIENTIFIC NAME: *Pterophylla camellifolia*

DESCRIPTION: The "true" katydid measures 1³/₄ to 2¹/₈ inches long. The light green forewings are convexly shaped and are crossed by many conspicuous veins.

HABITAT AND RANGE: A forest and woodland species, the range of the true katydid stretches from Massachusetts to Florida, and west to Texas and Kansas.

A famous children's verse went like this: "Katydid, o-she-did, katydid, did, she-did."

The song of the katydid was thought to predict the weather. In the United States it was believed that the first song of the katydid meant the frost was six weeks away. In Missouri it was believed that the song of the katydid meant it was time to plant corn, while in Kentucky, the first song of the katydid meant ninety days until frost.

A New England superstition suggested that the chirp of a katydid inside the house was an omen of death. In Maryland it was believed that to be bitten by a katydid would cause one to have fits.

In a Cherokee story two hunters camping in the woods heard the call of a katydid. One of them turned to the katydid and said, "What are you singing for? Don't you know you'll die before the season ends?"

The katydid answered, "You need not boast. You'll die before tomorrow night." The next day the hunters were surprised by the enemy, and the man who had mocked the katydid died in battle.

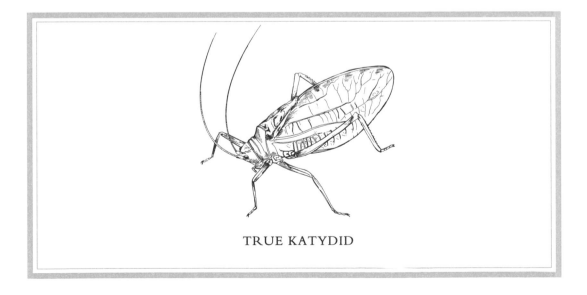

TRUE KATYDID

COMMON NAME: Ladybug, Two-spotted

SCIENTIFIC NAME: *Adalia bipunctata*

DESCRIPTION: This small beetle measures $^1/_8$ to $^1/_4$ inch long. The head and thorax are black with yellow markings. The back is orange with two large, conspicuous spots.

HABITAT AND RANGE: Common in fields, gardens, grasslands, and sometimes in houses throughout North America.

During the Middle Ages, ladybugs ate pests attacking grape vines and saved the grapes. They were dedicated to the Virgin Mary, "Our Lady," and received the common name Ladybug. In England they are called ladybird beetles. Other common names for this small beetle are fly-golding and God Almighty's cow.

Ladybugs were considered fortune tellers, particularly on matters of the heart. For exam-ple, if you put a ladybug on the back of your hand and recite, "Fly ladybug, north, south, east or west, Fly where the man is found that I love best," the ladybug will at least get you started in the right direction. If a ladybug flies away, rain is thought to be on the way. It is considered bad luck to kill a ladybug.

One of the most common children's rhymes is "Ladybug, ladybug, fly away home, your house is on fire and your children all

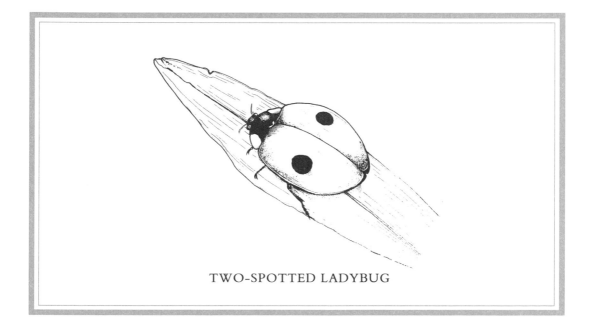

TWO-SPOTTED LADYBUG

gone." This rhyme is probably based on the fact that ladybugs feed on small insect pests such as aphids or scale, which infests hop vines. After the hops were harvested, the fields were burned to clear away the insect pests, and the young ladybugs were also destroyed since the immature forms do not have wings and are incapable of flying.

In German folklore the ladybug is a child-bringer. In other cultures, ladybugs were thought to hold the power to tell the time of day and forecast a long or short life.

In New England and Canada if a ladybug lands on your dress, you will soon get a new dress; if it lands on your hands, you will be getting new gloves.

The number of spots on the ladybug's shell was thought to indicate a good or poor harvest, or if you find one in the house, the number of spots will tell you how many dollars you will soon receive.

In India, England, and parts of the United States, it is considered bad luck to kill a ladybug because the souls of the dead are found within.

Various cultures used the ladybug for folk cures, including remedies for colic and measles. To cure a toothache, it was suggested that you take one or two ladybugs, smash them, and stuff them into the cavity of the tooth.

COMMON NAME: Mantis, Praying

SCIENTIFIC NAME: *Mantis religiosa*

DESCRIPTION: A large insect, the praying mantis measures 2 to 2 1/2 inches in length, including the wings. It is either green or brown. Front legs are held up in front as if in prayer. Antennae are short; the brown eyes are compound, turning darker at night.

HABITAT AND RANGE: Found on foliage in grasslands, meadows, and gardens throughout Europe and the eastern United States.

P raying mantis was introduced to the United States in 1899. It was seen as beneficial as it began preying on the gypsy moth caterpillars that were becoming a serious problem in the eastern states. The praying mantis is highly cannibalistic, though, and did not affect the caterpillar population drastically.

In the southern United States, there was a long-held belief that the praying mantis poisoned livestock. This is entirely unfounded because the mantis eats only other insects, not larger animals, and not even plants.

Mantis is from a Greek word that means "prophet, diviner, or seer," and was a name given to the insect because of its front "pray-

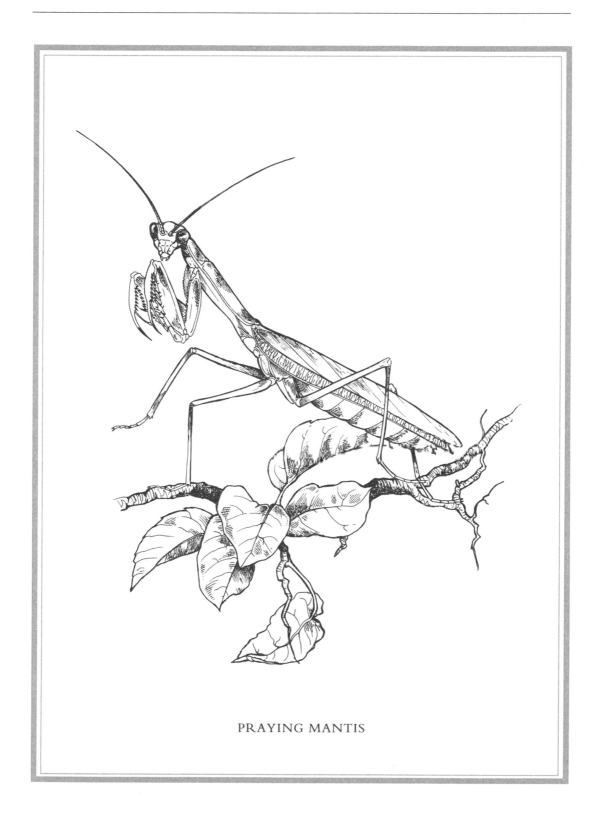

PRAYING MANTIS

ing" legs. The praying mantis is also known as "soothsayer" and "the devil's rearhorse."

One legend says that Saint Francis Xavier asked the praying mantis to sing praises to God. The insect responded by immediately singing a beautiful canticle.

Superstition holds that if you ask for directions from the praying mantis, it will hold up one leg or the other to indicate the correct way to go.

African bushmen consider the mantis a hero-god and a trickster. This insect was regarded with such respect that it was considered bad luck to say its name aloud. In other cultures, the mantis was believed to be concerned with conducting the souls of the dead through all the necessary gates to the underworld. Both Turks and Arabs believe that the mantis prays constantly with its face turned toward Mecca.

In China praying mantises were kept in small cages and were pitted against one another like fighting cocks.

COMMON NAME: Mosquito

SCIENTIFIC NAME: *Culex pipiens*

DESCRIPTION: This tiny insect measures 1/8 to 1/4 inch long. The thorax is light brown or gray; the abdomen has white bands. Two commonly found subspecies are named for their geographic range. One is the northern house mosquito, the other is the southern.

HABITAT AND RANGE: Mosquitoes live and breed near stagnant water, such as swamps or ponds, throughout the United States.

Indian tribes in British Columbia call the sun both Sacred One and Our Father. It was believed that the sun and a goddess named Alkuyntam created mankind. The mother of this goddess was a cannibal who was thought to have a long, mosquito-like snout she placed in people's ears to suck their blood out. According to this myth, when a cannibal's body is burned, the ashes turn into mosquitoes.

Similarly, a Rumanian superstition says mosquitoes were created from the smoke of the devil's pipe. Rumanians also suggest that angels cannot enter a house where mosquitoes are.

This pestering little insect was so prevalent in northeastern Honduras and eastern Nicaragua that early travelers named the tribes there the Miskitoes in reference to them. Mosquitoes in the area are said to be large enough and of such numbers to kill a man in a single night.

In the Chaco Indian myth, Moon came to

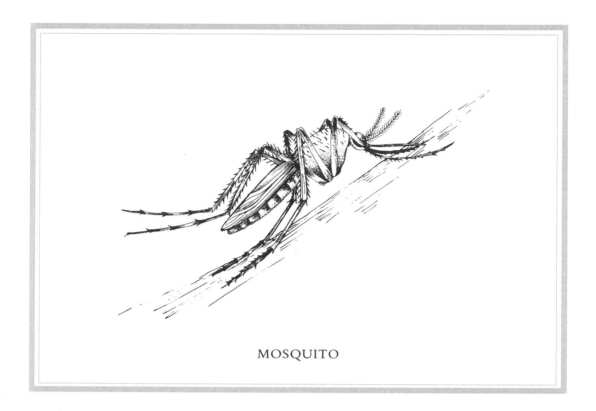

MOSQUITO

Mosquito's house and almost stepped on him, Mosquito bit him, and, according to legend, Moon died, only to be revived by Sun.

Ask a firefly why he carries a light, and he'll tell you it is so he can see Mosquito's dagger. The reason the male mosquito makes no sound is that he was put in jail for carrying a dagger and lost his voice while he was there.

In Newfoundland and Labrador it is thought that mosquitoes bite worst just before a storm.

Many folk superstitions suggest that if you hold your breath when a mosquito lands on you, he cannot pull out his stinger and thus will die.

An Algonquian Indian story says that long ago an Indian man named Pug-a-mah-kon was married to a lazy woman who never did anything to help him. One day the man heard that Wakonda, one of the Great Spirits,

was coming to visit. He begged his wife to clean his clothes, but she failed to do so. When Wakonda appeared, the man was standing with his dirty clothes in his arms. Wakonda told Pug-a-mah-kon to take some of the dirt clinging to the clothes and throw it at his lazy wife. He did this and wherever the clumps of dirt landed on the woman, they changed into mosquitoes.

The Japanese Ainu tell the tale that at one time there lived a terrible hobgoblin whose body was covered with hair. A young hunter came near his house one day, and when the hobgoblin appeared he shot an arrow directly into the monster's one eye and killed him. The hunter then burned the body and scattered the ashes, and the ashes all turned to gnats, mosquitoes, and gadflies. The young hunter said, better the lesser evil of these irritating insects than the great evil of the hobgoblin.

COMMON NAME: Moth, Luna

SCIENTIFIC NAME: *Actias luna*

DESCRIPTION: Iridescent green and yellow, the luna moth is one of the most beautiful of all moths. Its wingspan is 3 to 7 1/2 inches. Spots on the wings are often outlined with dark markings. Antennae resemble feathers.

HABITAT AND RANGE: Luna moths inhabit southeastern Canada and the eastern half of the United States and can be found wherever there are trees, often near lights.

A nineteenth-century superstition suggested that if a moth flies around you, you will receive a letter. The bigger the moth, the bigger the letter. If a moth flies around a lamp once, a postcard is coming, twice means a letter.

If a dark-winged moth flies toward the bed light, it is a sign of bad luck. If it is a light-winged moth, good luck will follow.

Clothes moths are called ghosts. If you kill one, you will injure a relative. During the seventeenth century in Europe, the oil taken from a clothes moth was used to cure warts, deafness, and leprosy.

A Welsh superstition suggests that when a witch dies, her soul passes into a large-winged moth.

The Cherokee tell of a small yellow moth that flies around the fire at night. When it finally flies too near and falls into the flame, they say that the moth is going to bed. Medicine men called on this small moth when curing diseases of the fire, such as sore eyes and frostbite.

The fat caterpillars called "wooly bears" are immature stages of a moth. In 1609 the naturalist Edward Topsell called these "Palmer worms." A "Palmer" was a wandering monk who had roving habits and a rather rugged appearance late in the season, characteristics that reminded Topsell of the wooly bear caterpillar.

The Tiger moth caterpillar has a band of reddish brown around its body. The width of this band indicated the severity of the coming winter. A wide band means a mild winter.

LUNA MOTH

COMMON NAME: Scorpion

SCIENTIFIC NAME: *Centruroides sp.*

DESCRIPTION: These scorpions look like miniature lobsters with pinchers. These species are dark brown or tan, sometimes showing greenish yellow stripes. The slender abdomen is constricted at each segment.

HABITAT AND RANGE: Scorpions prefer dark spaces and can be found in rocky crevices or under stones or bark. Their range extends from Florida and the Gulf States, west to Arizona and Mexico.

The scorpion's sting was believed to be fatal to women and children but was thought to be harmful to men only in the morning when it first emerges from its hole. According to Pliny, the mother scorpion produces eleven offspring at a time and kills all but one, which escapes death by perching on her haunches. The surviving offspring then avenges his siblings' death by killing the mother.

According to a thirteenth-century manuscript, the scorpion is a kind of serpent with a face like a woman's. It practices deception with its head, stings with its tail, and is representative of lechery. For many ages, scorpions have been symbolic of death and destruction, envy and hate.

The theme of the scorpion is important in Egyptian mythology. The goddess Isis was once accompanied on a dangerous journey by seven scorpions, the leader of which was called Tefen. The Egyptian goddess Selkis, also known as Selket or Serquet, was the scorpion goddess, a manifestation of the scorching heat of the sun. Her role, along with the goddesses Isis, Nephthys, and Neit, was to guard the viscera that had been removed from bodies during mummification. Seth, an Upper Egyptian god, had only evil sides to his nature and was often associated with scorpions.

In Sumeria scorpions were thought to guard the gateway to the sun. In Babylonia the scorpion was considered one of the monsters created by Tiamat and was a symbol of darkness and the setting sun.

The scorpion is a southern constellation and the eighth sign of the zodiac. According to mythology, Scorpio stung Orion to death and scared the horses while Phaeton tried to drive the sun chariot. Scorpio is of special significance to the people of New Zealand. They call this constellation the Fish Hook of Maui because it supposedly fished up their island from the bottom of the sea.

In Kings 12:11 in the Old Testament, scorpions symbolize the wilderness, desolation, and danger.

Pliny suggested that the only cure for a scorpion sting was to drink a concoction of wine mixed with the roasted body of a scorpion. An old folk superstition said that if you were stung by a scorpion and survived, you would not be bothered by wasp, bee, or hornet stings.

SCORPION

COMMON NAME: Spider, Garden

SCIENTIFIC NAME: *Araneus diadematus*

DESCRIPTION: Males are noticeably smaller than the females, measuring only $^1/_4$ to $^3/_8$ inch as opposed to the female, which is $^3/_4$ to $1^1/_8$ inches long. The abdomen is rounded and shows yellow or orange markings on black.

HABITAT AND RANGE: True to its name, the garden spider inhabits foliage or shrubbery in grasslands, meadows, and gardens through out the United States. It is somewhat rare in the Rocky Mountain areas.

"I don't know how the first spider in the early days of the world happened to think up this fancy idea of spinning a web, but she did, and it was clever of her, too. And since then, all of us spiders have had to work the same trick."

—Charlotte, in *Charlotte's Web* by E.B. White.

According to Native American legend, when the earth was first made there was no sun, so the animals gathered together and decided to steal the sun. All tried and failed until Grandmother Spider tried. Instead of trying to hold onto the sun herself, she wove a web, put a piece of the sun in the web, and brought it back to earth.

When she returned, the animals decided that the sun should be high in the sky so all could see it. The buzzard offered to take the sun up high in the sky and, putting it on top of his head where his feathers were thickest, flew high, high in the sky. He finally took it to the top of the sky, but the sun was so hot, it burned all the feathers off the top of his head.

Another version of this catching-the-sun

story says that Grandmother Spider made a tiny bowl from clay and carried it with her all the way to the sun, spinning a fine thread behind her so she could find her way back. When she reached the sun, she took a piece of it and put it in her small bowl and returned to the other animals. Even today the spider web is shaped like the sun with its rays, and the spider always spins her web early in the morning before the sun is fully awake.

American Indians believed that when a person died, he climbed up to the heavens on ropes of spider silk. The Apache honored Grandfather Spider, for it was he who made a ladder of sunbeams so they might beam up from the center of the earth.

The Hopi believed Grandmother Spider was messenger of the sun spirit, and the Cherokee believed that Grandmother Spider brought the first fire into the world by snatching a bit of the sun. The Chippewa hung real spider webs on the hoops of a baby's cradleboard so any harm floating in the air would be caught in the web.

Some African tribes looked upon the spider as a national hero and believed it to be shrewd, designing, and a selfish trickster. An

GARDEN SPIDER

Ethiopian proverb says that "When spider webs unite, they can tie up a lion."

According to a Greek myth, there once lived a maiden named Arachne whose special gift was that she could weave something out of anything. In her cradle, she wove the sunbeams, and as she grew she continued to weave until she could make cloth that was light and beautiful, and she became known as Arachne the spinner.

As her skills increased, Arachne became more and more boastful about her weaving ability until finally even the gods on Mount Olympus heard her. One night Arachne

heard something scratch at her windowsill and she thought it was a branch. She opened the window, and a bent old woman walked in. The old woman suggested to Arachne that she and Minerva, the goddess of weaving and spinning, have a contest.

The next morning Minerva herself appeared at her door and the contest began. Minerva worked with the colors of the heavens, and Arachne chose the colors of the earth. Arachne wove in stories of the gods and goddesses looking foolish and defeated. By nightfall the contest was over. When Minerva turned and saw Arachne's weaving, she became incensed at the affront to the gods and goddesses and, in a rage, turned Arachne into a spider and said that she would continue to weave her magic all of her life.

Romans believed they could tell the future by watching a spider move within its web. They believed that spiders were fortune-tellers and bringers of fortune as well.

A Danish fable tells about a spider who built a wonderful web in a barn. He began high up at the top of the barn and spun a single long thread all the way down to one of the beams. Then he began crisscrossing silken threads like the spokes of a wheel, working until the web was large and intricate and beautiful.

Looking at his beautiful web happily, he said to himself, "This will catch many fat flies." Then he happened to see the single long thread from the top of the barn.

"Well, I wonder why I built that. It won't catch any flies," he said, and without thinking snipped that long single strand. No sooner had he done this than the entire beautiful web collapsed.

Spiders have long been thought to be able to predict the weather, as is evidenced in the following favorite sayings:

"If you kill a spider, a storm is sure to follow."
"When a spider spins its web before noon, sunny weather's coming soon."
"If spiders abandon their webs, a storm is on the way."
"If spiders on the air do fly, the spell will soon be very dry."

Other spider sayings warn of other situations, such as "If a spider falls into the fire, a witch is waiting nearby." Sometimes spiders bring good news:

"Spider in the corner, money in the chest."
"If a spider crawls into your pocket, you will always have money."
"A spider hanging overhead means you will get a letter."
"If you walk into a spiderweb, you will meet a friend that day."
"If a spider creeps across you, it is measuring you for new clothes."
"A spider at night brings joy and delight, A spider seen in the morning brings you a warning."

"If you wish to live and thrive, Let a spider run alive" probably originated with the myth that a spider spun a web over the manger where the Christ Child was born to protect him from danger.

Of course, some questions about the spider, originating with Mary Howitt, have been asked for many years. "Will you walk into my parlor?" said the spider to the fly. "Tis the prettiest parlor that ever you did spy."

The old English word for spider was *attercop*, meaning "poisonhead." Our word cobweb comes from this.

For centuries folk healers have prescribed spiders and spiderwebs as medicine. Dr. Thomas Muffet was a physician who recommended swallowing spiders as a cure for various illnesses and practiced some of these on his unfortunate daughter. From this came the nursery rhyme,

"There came a big spider,
And sat down beside her,
And frightened Miss Muffet away."

Spider webs were wrapped around cuts to keep them from bleeding. Swallowing a ball of spiders' webs was said to cure asthma. Allowing spiders to run about freely was thought to prevent gout.

REPTILES
AND
AMPHIBIANS

COMMON NAME: Alligator, American

SCIENTIFIC NAME: *Alligator mississippiensis*

DESCRIPTION: The largest North American reptile, the alligator has a broad, rounded snout. From the snout to the tip of the tail, the elongated body measures from 6 to 15 feet. It has brownish gray, thick skin, checkered on top, almost spotted underneath. Young are only 9 inches long when born; they are black with yellow crossbands.

HABITAT AND RANGE: Alligators live in fresh or brackish waters, such as swamps, ponds, and rivers, in both coastal and inland areas from southeastern North Carolina south through Florida and west to Texas and southern Arkansas.

The name alligator comes from the Spanish, *el largato*, "the lizard." Alligator teeth, which are hollow, were used to dip up a measured amount of gunpowder. In Louisiana, a bagful of alligator teeth was thought to prevent warts. Rubbing oil from the alligator on a person's skin was thought to ease the pain of rheumatism, and ashes from a burned alligator skin were thought to produce a narcotic effect.

The use of the word alligator to mean "friend" or "acquaintance" became famous in the expression, "See you later, alligator." The correct response was "After while, crocodile."

In the southeastern United States, a particularly masculine man was referred to as an alligator.

Uncle Remus tells a tale of why the alligator's back is rough:

One day Bre'r Rabbit is being chased by a dog, and he runs and runs until he is out of breath. Finally he comes to the creek where Bre'r Gator is sunning himself. Bre'r Gator asks Bre'r Rabbit why he is out of breath and Bre'r Rabbit tells him that Trouble is chasing him, in the form of the dog. Bre'r Gator just laughs and laughs and tells Bre'r Rabbit that if trouble ever chased *him*, he'd just turn around and shake his hand and ask him how he was doing. This advice makes Bre'r Rabbit mad and when a little while later Bre'r Gator falls asleep in the broom grass, Bre'r Rabbit sets fire to the grass. Bre'r Gator wakes with fire all around and calls out to Bre'r Rabbit, "Trouble! Trouble!" but Bre'r Rabbit just laughs. Soon Bre'r Gator comes running through the burning grass, his back on fire, and throws himself on his back to put out the flames, swiveling this way and that, so that even today the alligator's back is rough from the day he had to run through Bre'r Rabbit's fire.

The Choctaw Indians tell this tale of how the alligator taught their people to hunt:

A Choctaw hunter always had very bad luck while hunting, in spite of the fact that he was skilled and had strong, straight arrows. He

AMERICAN ALLIGATOR

finally decided that he would succeed at hunting or lose his life trying. He hunted for three days until he came upon a dried up pond, in the center of which was an alligator stranded in the mud and unable to move for lack of water. The hunter took pity on the alligator and helped it to water. In return, the alligator gave the man these instructions on how to become a great hunter: *You will soon meet a young doe. Do not kill it, for it is not even old enough to have young yet. Then you will meet a large doe, but do not kill her either, for she will have many fawns. Next you will meet a young buck, but do not kill him, for he will father many fawns. Finally you will meet a large buck whose time on Earth will be nearly up. Kill this buck quickly and mercifully, asking forgiveness and offering thanks.*

The hunter did as he was instructed and soon became the greatest hunter of the tribe. He taught all his people how to hunt in this manner, and as long as they followed his teachings, the Choctaw were never hungry.

COMMON NAME: Chameleon, American (Green Anole)
SCIENTIFIC NAME: *Anolis carolinensis*

DESCRIPTION: The only chameleon native to the United States is the green anole, characterized by the conspicuous pink or red throat fan displayed by the males. Like chameleons in Africa, the color of this small lizard changes with varying light and temperature and the animal's emotional state. Males are highly territorial. Large toe pads facilitate climbing.

HABITAT AND RANGE: A species of the southern states, green anoles are found as far north as North Carolina, south to Florida, and west to Oklahoma and eastern Texas and in the Caribbean Islands. They sleep high in trees and are seen most often on fences, trees, shrubs, and vines.

The word chameleon comes from two Greek words—*chamai*, meaning "on the ground," and *leon*, meaning "lion." The chameleon may look like a lion as it stalks prey, but almost all chameleon species dwell in trees and not on the ground. Aristotle wrote one of the first descriptions of the chameleon, saying that it could change colors as easily as a man changes moods.

Because of their unusual appearance and their ability to change colors, chameleons were thought to hold supernatural powers. It was considered bad luck to kill a chameleon since it was believed capable of housing the spirit of a dead ancestor.

Chameleon parts figured largely in several country concoctions. For instance, one folk recipe suggested that the left foot of a chameleon cooked with certain plants would make one invisible. In Africa, as protection against robbers, the foreleg of a chameleon was put into a hyena skin and worn on the left arm. Another superstition said that the head, throat,

and liver of a chameleon burned along with hard wood would bring rain. Pliny's *Natural History,* written in A.D. 77, said that a green lizard caught live, put in a vessel, and worn as an amulet would cure recurring fevers.

Captured chameleons have been known to go weeks without food, giving rise to the superstition that these little lizards live on air. The poet Shelley wrote, "chameleons feed on light and air," and Shakespeare wrote in *Hamlet* about air being the "chameleon's dish."

A sixteenth-century folktale tells of a serpent who was preparing to eat a chameleon it had captured. The chameleon suddenly blew itself up into a large balloon shape and put a stick into its mouth crosswise, and the serpent could not eat him.

An African folktale tells how the chameleon became king. All the animals were sitting around one day when the current king, Lion, ambled up and sat down among them. "I don't want to be king anymore," Lion told the animals. "It's lonely on the throne with no

AMERICAN CHAMELEON

one to talk to. Let's have a race to see who should be king."

The animals were excited because everyone wanted to be king. They all lined up to race to the throne to see who would be the new king. The cunning chameleon knew that the cheetah was the fastest animal and would probably win, so he quietly crept onto the cheetah's tail and hung on for dear life. The cheetah did reach the throne first, and just as he was preparing to sit down and become king, the chameleon jumped off his tail and sat on the throne. The animals were amazed, but they believed chameleon had won the race and made him their new king. After a few days, chameleon was sorry he had won the race, for he, too, found out how lonely it was to sit all alone on the throne.

Another African tale tells how God sent two animals to earth with messages about death. The chameleon was to tell people that they would be born again after death, and the lizard was to say that after death there would be only nothingness. The lizard was the first to arrive on earth, and he promptly told his bad news. By the time the chameleon arrived with the good news, the people were so depressed that they took their anger out on the chameleon for being late and are still angry to this day. In Nyasaland it is customary to kill chameleons with tobacco juice.

To be "as faithful as the chameleon's skin" is a sarcastic reference to untrustworthiness, since the chameleon is always changing the color of its skin.

COMMON NAME: Crocodile

SCIENTIFIC NAME: *Crocodylus acutus*

DESCRIPTION: A reptile similar to the American alligator but with a long, slender snout.

HABITAT AND RANGE: Very rare inhabitant of swamps in the Florida Keys.

How cheerfully he seems to grin
How neatly spreads his claws,
And welcomes little fishes in,
With greatly smiling jaws.

—Lewis Carroll

The following story is told in India about a crocodile and a monkey:

A monkey lived high in the trees next to a river full of crocodiles. A mother crocodile was becoming more and more frustrated with her son because he was not very smart. One day she said to him, "Go to the trees on the riverbank and get me a monkey's heart to eat. That's all I want for breakfast— just a monkey's heart."

The young crocodile was puzzled and did not know how to get a monkey's heart, but he wanted to please his mother so he scooted up onto the land and offered to take the monkey across the river where sweeter fruits grew. The monkey agreed and climbed onto the crocodile's back. Halfway across, the crocodile said, "Foolish monkey, now I will get your heart to give to my mother." The wily monkey

replied, "Foolish crocodile, I left my heart at home. Take me back, and I'll fetch it for you." The crocodile turned and returned to the river bank. The monkey jumped off and ran into the forest, never to be seen again.

The term "crocodile tears" is from a medieval legend that suggested that crocodiles wept for the men they slew and ate. The tears are thought to be tears not of repentance but of frustration that there is so little flesh on the head.

Crocodiles were important to the Egyptians, who believed them to be sources of revelation and embalmed them when they died. They fed crocodile meat to the god Souchos, who was a crocodile himself.

In Africa it was thought that crocodiles carried the souls of dead relatives. If a person was attacked by a crocodile, it was thought to be an act of vengeance by the dead person inhabiting the crocodile.

According to Egyptian superstition, he who kills a crocodile becomes a crocodile.

So powerful was the crocodile that the Bantu tribe of Africa shunned anyone even splashed by this animal. Other African tribes

AMERICAN CROCODILE

believed that the crocodile could grab a man's shadow and pull him into the water. A South African Vandau proverb says that "the strength of the crocodile is in the water."

The name crocodile means "gravel worm," from the two Greek words *kroke*, meaning "gravel," and *drilos*, meaning "worm."

The Chiriqui Indians of Panama depict the crocodile god as having the legs and body of a human and the head of a crocodile.

COMMON NAME: Frog (Bullfrog)

SCIENTIFIC NAME: *Rana catesbeiana*

DESCRIPTION: The largest frog species in North America, bullfrogs measure 3 1/2 to 8 inches long and have smooth olive green or brown skin marked with splotches on the back and bands on the legs. Coloration lightens to pale green on the head. A ridge or band of skin extends from the eye around the eardrum.

HABITAT AND RANGE: Bullfrogs can be found in any permanent body of water from the Atlantic Coast west to Colorado and New Mexico, north to Canada, and south to Mexico. This amphibian is also found in many areas along the West Coast.

"A discovery!
On my frog's smooth green belly
there sits no button."

—Yaku

Because frogs are often seen in great numbers as it begins to rain, they have long been credited as rain-bringers and are also symbolic of fecundity and fertility. The Egyptian goddess Hekt, or Hequat, was the Frog Goddess, who had power over the water and was considered protectress of mothers and newborn babies. The Mayan and Aztec Indian cultures also recognized a frog deity.

Early Christians used the frog as a symbol of new birth, though it later came to be symbolic of sin and greed. In Chinese symbolism, the lunar yin is represented by a frog, and a frog pictured in a well was thought to symbolize a person of limited vision and understanding.

Several folk superstitions have developed around the frog. One old folk superstition suggested that the tongue of a live frog placed over your wife's beating heart while she sleeps would act as a truth drug. It was also thought that if you killed a frog, your cow would die. Another belief is that a wish made when you hear the first frog of spring will come true. An old superstition among gamblers is that if you come across a frog on your way to the card game, you will have good luck.

The story of the frog prince is a beast-and-human marriage folktale told in India, Hungary, Norway, Germany, and the British Isles. One versions tells about the youngest of three princesses who drops her golden ball into a well. A frog finds it and returns it to her in exchange for her promise to be his companion and eat and sleep with him.

Once the princess has her ball again, though, she ignores the frog and runs back to the castle. That night, when the entire court is at dinner, the small frog, who has hopped all the way from the well, knocks at the door. He tells the King about the princess's promise, and the king insists that the girl keep her promise. She makes a face and kisses the frog, who then turns into a handsome prince. A

AMERICAN BULLFROG

modern variation of this story has the moral, "You have to kiss a lot of frogs before you find a prince."

An Australian aboriginal legend tells of Tiddalick, a giant frog "so big that his shadow turned day into night, so powerful that his voice drowned the thunder, and so heavy that a single hop shook the ground for miles and miles around," according to Susan Nunes' book, *Tiddalick the Frog.*

According to this legend Tiddalick wakes up grumpy one morning and begins to drink all the water on the earth until finally he has drunk it all up and the plants begin to die and the animals plead with him to release the water. Tiddalick, still grumpy, refuses to do this.

The animals are at their wits' ends, not knowing how to get Tiddalick to release the water. They finally decide that if they can get him to laugh, he might do just that. They send a tiny eel to dance before Tiddalick, and soon the frog begins to laugh so hard that the water runs out of his mouth into the parched ground, and the earth begins to bloom once again. (The Andamanese tell a similar story about the toad.)

Northwestern Indian cultures tell a legend about Frog and Mink (considered a companion of Raven, the Trickster figure). Mink, called Born-to-be-the-Sun, decided he wanted to marry Frog. His mother asked if he would not become tired of her croaking, but

Mink said no, that's what he liked about frogs. So he married a frog wife, and all the frogs croaked in celebration. Soon Mink could no longer stand the croaking, and he returned to his mother, who shook her head and said, "Didn't I tell you?"

Many folk cures for thrush rely on frogs or toads. The placement of a frog in the patient's mouth was thought to cure the dis-ease. An old Yorkshire cure for whooping cough was to make soup from nine frogs without allowing the patient to see the frogs or to know the soup's ingredients.

An American Indian woman wanting to avoid pregnancy would catch a frog and spit in its face three times.

It is said that frogs are like gossips—they drink and talk.

COMMON NAME: Gecko, Western Banded

SCIENTIFIC NAME: *Coleonyx variegatus*

DESCRIPTION: All three species of banded geckos (western, Texas banded, and barefoot gecko) have vertical pupils and movable eyelids, characteristics that make it easy to distinguish them from other species. The western banded gecko measures 2 to 3 inches long and has cream or pinkish skin with dark brown bands or spots along the length of the body. As the gecko ages (or in certain environments), these bands break up into splotches. The male has a prominent spur on each side of the tail.

HABITAT AND RANGE: This lizard is found in chaparral and desert areas in the extreme Southwest.

A tokay, a particular kind of gecko, is considered a good luck omen An American folktale relates why the gecko and other lizards cannot sit down. When lizards were first made, they used to sit like frogs or dogs, with their feet out in front of them. One day the lizard and the frog were trying to squeeze through a crack in a split-rail fence. The frog said, "I'll get through this crack, God willing," and squeezed through. The feisty lizard said, "I'll get through this crack, God willing or not," but even though he tried and tried, he could not get through. Suddenly the rail fell down on him and squished him flat, and since that day he hasn't been able to sit down.

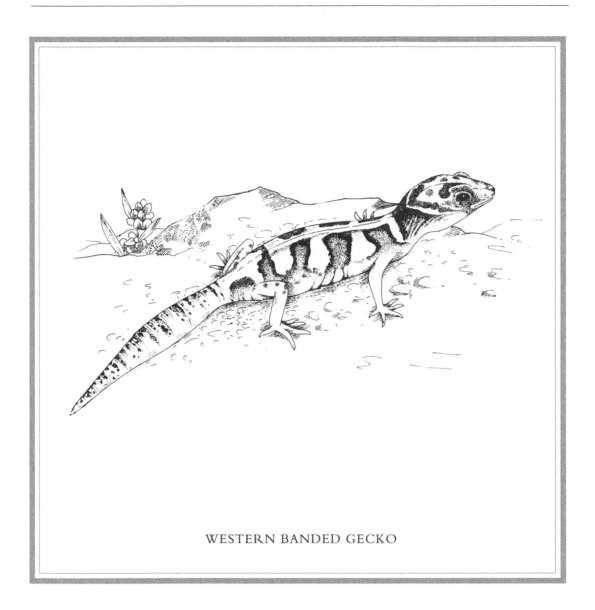

WESTERN BANDED GECKO

COMMON NAME: Gila Monster

SCIENTIFIC NAME: *Heloderma suspectum*

DESCRIPTION: The only poisonous lizards found in North America are the Mexican beaded lizard and the gila monster. The latter has a thick, heavy body measuring 9 to 14 inches in length, with a short, wide tail and a brightly colored body of black and pink, orange, or yellow. The dark tongue is forked.

HABITAT AND RANGE: From Utah and Colorado south to New Mexico and southern California, gila monsters are found in shrubby or grassy areas, canyons, or arroyos.

Among the Navajo, the gila monster is thought to be the first medicine man. When Navajo medicine men begin a curing ceremony, they sprinkle sacred pollen in the four directions, chanting special prayers to gila monster. The gila monster, with his protective coat of hard scales, was thought to lend its protective coat to those who were ill.

It was thought that when the gila monster walked, his foreleg would sometimes tremble, and it was believed that from this trembling he could foretell the coming of a mortal illness.

Flint, a sacred stone to the Navajo, was thought to be like the protective armor of the gila monster, and a special ceremony called the Flintway was performed to invoke protective powers.

Protected by law in Arizona, the gila monster is named for Arizona's Gila River.

Along with its cousin, the Mexican bearded lizard, the skin of the gila monster looks like Indian beadwork. Its tail serves to store fat that the animal uses during times when food is unavailable, and its bite, which is poisonous, is deathly to small animals. Raymond L. Ditmas wrote in *Reptiles of the World* in 1910 that it was "A highly dangerous brute to tamper with . . . ."

Many American Indian tribes believed that this lizard held great powers and considered it an omen of evil. Among its supposed magic was the ability of this lizard to influence the weather and to leap as high as a human hand to bite.

The Apache Indians believed that black smoke came from its mouth and that its breath was so poisonous that all vegetation it touched would turn dark and die.

GILA MONSTER

COMMON NAME: Iguana, Desert

SCIENTIFIC NAME: *Dipsosaurus dorsalis*

DESCRIPTION: This lizard has a round, pale-colored body, a long tail, and a small, rounded head. The scales are small and overlap on the belly. It measures 4 to 5 $^3/_4$ inches in length.

HABITAT AND RANGE: This lizard lives in creosote-bush deserts and prefers temperatures above 100 degrees Fahrenheit. The ability to withstand such high temperatures is advantageous because other animals are rarely active during midday in the desert when the iguana comes out, thus reducing its risk from predators and competition for food. Desert iguana is found in desert areas of the southwestern United States and northwestern Mexico.

Like all lizards, iguanas are believed to be messengers of the gods. In the Philippines, for example, it was believed that if the big iguana came into a house, someone in the house was summoned to die.

In a modern African fairy tale from Forbes Suart's book *The Magic Horn*, the hyena finds a pair of jeweled sandals in the sand one day. He builds himself a throne of mud, hangs the sandals from his ears, and proclaims himself king. All the animals pay tribute to this strange creature on the mud throne until the iguana comes along. Instead of paying homage, the iguana calls him a ragged impostor. The hyena tries to catch the iguana, who swims swiftly to his burrow, turning only to tell the hyena: "King of nothing, tattered hyena, tumbled by the fat iguana."

An Australian legend tells about the old days when the snake was harmless and the iguana had a poisonous bite. The iguana, which was big and powerful during those days, had an insatiable appetite for the flesh of blackfellows, which he would slay in great numbers. All the tribes came together and said that something must be done about this monster, but no one wanted to risk getting killed. Finally the snake said he would sneak up and capture the bag of poison that made the iguana so powerful. He crept up to the iguana and cleverly tricked him into letting him hold the bag of poison. As soon as the snake had hold of the bag, he scooted off back to the tribes. They were amazed and said to the snake, "Give us the bag of poison so that we can destroy it," but the snake said, "No, now I have the poison, and I am the most powerful animal." Since that time the iguana has had no poison.

DESERT IGUANA

COMMON NAME: Lizard, Common Collared

SCIENTIFIC NAME: *Crotaphytus collaris*

DESCRIPTION: This lizard is 3 to 4¹/₂ inches long with a broad head. Two black and white rings are found on its neck, and many spots and stripes are on its brightly colored body, which can be green, olive, yellow, bluish, or brown, depending on each lizard's particular habitat. Males are usually brighter in color than females, though the latter form bright spots of orange on the sides of the body and neck during mating season in spring. (For information on other types of lizards—chameleons, geckos, gila monsters, iguanas, and skinks—see the individual entries for these animals.)

HABITAT AND RANGE: The collared lizard prefers areas with little vegetation, rocky hills, plateaus, canyons, and gullies. Its range includes eastern Utah and Colorado, east to Illinois, and south through Texas, New Mexico, and Arizona.

In every country where lizards are found, folklore about them is prevalent. Many cultures claim that the hand of man was fashioned after that of the lizard; others say that the first men were lizards. Lizards have been used to symbolize various principles and are considered omens of various events. In some cultures, the lizard is seen as a deity incarnate or the form in which the souls of dead relatives take refuge.

Lizards were often used in magical concoctions to rejuvenate the old, presumably because, like snakes, lizards discard their old skins to grow new ones. Roman myths depict the lizard as a symbol of death and rebirth because it was believed at that time that lizards slept all winter and awakened in spring.

In the American Southwest, people sometimes believed that lizards, who served as protective guardians, lived underneath houses. The occupants would sometimes leave milk and crumbs for the lizards, greeting them with delight when they appeared above ground.

In the Andaman Islands, myths indicate that the First Man was a monitor lizard, an amazing animal that could swim in water, walk on land, and climb trees; thus the monitor lizard was the symbolic master of the worlds of air, water, and land.

An Amazon Indian tribe believed that the lizard was a manifestation of Desana, the Master of Animals and Fish.

An Australian myth relates that the First Ancestor created many small black lizards, divided their feet into fingers and toes, made them noses, eyes, and mouths, and tried to stand them upright. Their tails were too long, however, so the First Ancestor cut off the tails, and then they were men. Another Australian belief was that the lizard was a culture hero who taught people the art of tattooing.

In Malaysia lizards were associated with childbirth and fertility. It was believed that if a lizard ran across a woman's skirt, she would

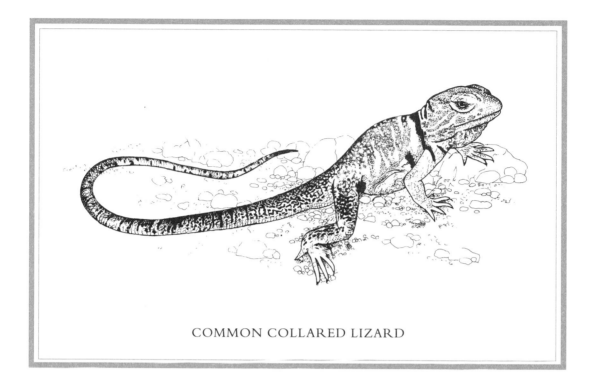

COMMON COLLARED LIZARD

soon conceive. Another superstition held that the lizard brings new babies into the world and helps their souls to enter into them.

In the Polynesian Islands, where these reptiles are greatly respected, the lizard cult is very common. In Polynesia, it was thought that the "dream soul" took the form of a lizard, thus it was extremely bad luck to kill a lizard that might be a loved one who was only dreaming.

Some primitive cultures kept lizards in cages because it was believed that they offered protection from thunder and lightning. In India, the lizard was a charm for luck, cures, and love. Arabs believed that a lizard in the hand was an aphrodisiac; they also thought that the lizard used medicinally would cure old men of impotence.

Ancient peoples believed the lizard did not have a tongue and was therefore symbolic of silence. In both Egyptian and Greek myth, the lizard symbolized wisdom and good fortune. Some European cultures considered the lizard a symbol of logic.

The following story tells how Sir Monitor Lizard obtained a wife:

Sir Monitor Lizard was fishing one day when he saw a piece of black wood floating. He picked it up and took it home, placing it on his mantelpiece to dry. He sat down to make an arrow, and as he worked, he heard someone laugh. He turned and saw that the wood had turned into a woman, who became his wife.

In Ireland it was believed that if one caught a lizard and licked all its body parts—

head, back, belly, and so on—this person's tongue would have the power to take the sting and pain out of a burn.

In the Alsace region, if a lizard ran across a woman's hand, it was believed she would become skillful at needlework.

During the eighteenth century, when exploration and adventures were in high fashion, the lizard was believed to be helpful to the traveler. According to *The Voyages, Dangerous Adventures, and Imminent Escapes of*

Captain Richard Falconer, published in 1720, lizards would awaken travelers by tickling them behind the ear, warning them of approaching danger from alligators, vipers, or other dangerous beasts.

A Somerset superstition claimed that one would have bad luck if one saw a lizard run across the road. The Aranda people never kill a lizard because they believe that if they do, the sky will fall down on the earth.

COMMON NAME: Newt, Eastern

SCIENTIFIC NAME: *Notophthalmus viridescens*

DESCRIPTION: Eastern newts are amphibians in the salamander family, but they lack the side grooves found on most other salamanders. The adult is olive green or brown, with a yellow belly showing numerous black dots. The length is 5 1/2 inches. The larvae remain in the water for several months until they lose their gills and transform into efts, the terrestrial stage of the newt's life. In this stage, the newt is red with dark spots evenly spaced down the back. The adults return to the water to live.

HABITAT AND RANGE: These newts are found throughout the eastern half of the United States and southeastern Canada. Adults are found in any calm, fresh water where vegetation is plentiful. Efts are found in moist, wooded areas.

An English phrase, "to be as overtired as a newt," is a euphemism used when someone is suffering from too much drink. According to P. B. and J. S. Medawar's book, *Aristotle to Zoos* , this expression can be attributed to "the somewhat tipsy-looking side-to-side movement of the newt's relatively big head, produced by its sigmoid swimming movements."

The witches in Shakespeare's *Macbeth* used

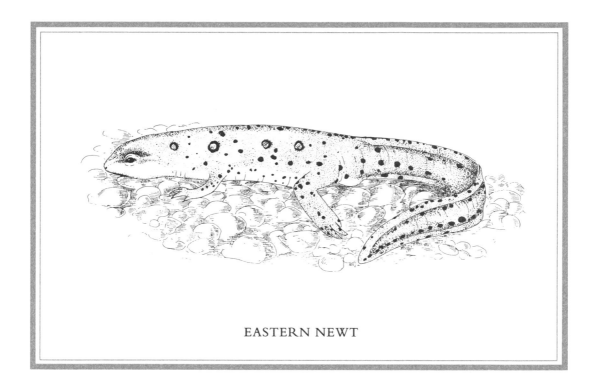

EASTERN NEWT

the newt in concocting their evil brew. In Act IV, scene one, the second witch chants:

"Eye of newt and toe of frog,
Wool of bat and tongue of dog,
Adder's fork and blind-worm sting,

Lizard's leg and howlet's wing,
For a charm of powerful trouble,
Like a hell-broth boil and bubble."

Newts seemed to add just the right touch to this brew.

COMMON NAME: Salamander, Tiger

SCIENTIFIC NAME: *Ambystoma tigrinum*

DESCRIPTION: The length of a salamander is difficult to determine because parts of the tail are often lost. Generally, however, this species of salamander measures 8 to 12 inches. Large, dark and light splotches run along the length of its body. It has a broad head and long, stout legs.

HABITAT AND RANGE: Tiger salamanders have a wide range, stretching from the shores of the Atlantic to the eastern edges of the Pacific coast states. They are not found in New England or Appalachian areas. The habitat of this amphibian is diverse as well, ranging from plains to forests. Salamanders can be found in almost any kind of still water from temporary rain puddles to lakes and ponds.

Salamanders were at one time considered highly poisonous. One superstition suggested that salamanders were so toxic they could wind themselves around the trunk of a fruit tree and poison all the fruit so that it would kill anyone who ate it.

The skins of salamanders were believed to be so cold that these small animals could crawl through fire without feeling the heat and even put out the flames. The skin was thought to be covered with hairs, and it was once believed that asbestos was made from this substance.

T. H. White wrote that an emperor of India had a fireproof suit made from a thousand salamander skins. Pliny wrote that the salamander searches for the hottest fire in which to breed, then puts it out with the coldness of its body. It was also believed that salamanders seek out blacksmiths' fires because they are so hot.

TIGER SALAMANDER

The Japanese dry salamanders and eat them in a concoction used to rid the body of worms. The Cherokee held the belief that if you ate the meat of the salamander and went into the fields soon after, all the crops would die.

In heraldry, salamanders symbolize courage.

COMMON NAME: Skink, Five-lined

SCIENTIFIC NAME: *Eumeces fasciatus*

DESCRIPTION: This lizard measures 5 to 8 inches long. Adults have faded lines the length of the body. The young have blue tails and yellow lines on their heads. Breeding males exhibit orange or red on the head.

HABITAT AND RANGE: Often found in gardens or near woods with abundant forest litter, skinks are also often seen basking in the sun on stumps or garden walls. Found in the eastern United States from New England south to Georgia and west to Oklahoma and Texas.

With more than 800 species, skinks form the largest family of lizards. Skinks can store fat in their tails for use during times when food is scarce.

Scincus scincus lives in northern Africa and is called a sandfish because of the way it looks when it is burrowing through sand. This species is sometimes called the "pharmacist's skink" because it was used medicinally. Arabs roasted the skink, ground the meat, and added it to chopped dates for a special delicacy.

The three-toed skink, *Chalcides striatus*, is found in southern France, Portugal, and Spain and was believed to be poisonous. It is called Seps from the Greek word that means "evil repute."

FIVE-LINED SKINK

SNAKES

Snakes are reptiles without limbs, ear openings, or movable eyelids. They have a single row of scales on their bellies. Snakes hear by detecting vibrations through the ground and smell by picking up particles of dust with their forked tongues. Often used as a symbol of death and immortality, snakes have been used to symbolize many opposing principles and have been considered both male and female. Joseph Campbell wrote that "Serpents seem to incarnate the elementary mystery of life wherever apparent opposites are cojoined."

In Egypt, the monster serpent Apop is a symbol of evil, but the royal serpent, the cobra, was worn on the head of the god Ra and represented supreme power and wisdom. In the Christian religion, the serpent is synonymous with Satan, while in other religions it is worshipped.

The name serpent is from the Sanskrit *sarpati*, meaning "the creeper." Although the words serpent and snake are often used interchangeably, the former most often refers to a poisonous snake.

In the days of ancient Greece and Rome, snakes were often kept in households and were associated with the gods and goddesses responsible for healing, particularly Asclepios, the god of medicine. This god was often shown carrying a staff or rod with a snake coiled around it. This symbol was eventually combined with the caduceus, the staff carried by Hermes, or Mercury, messenger to the gods. Hermes became associated with health and healing, and the two symbols joined to form the modern emblem of the caduceus, a staff with two intertwining snakes facing each other at the top. This emblem is used today as the insignia of physicians.

Snakes were chosen as a symbol for healing from the ancient belief that certain species could stop the Bubonic Plague. Although the ancient Greeks and Romans did not know of the connection between disease and the presence of rats and fleas, they did observe that places free from rats and abundant with snakes (which ate the rats) were healthier than those where rodents were numerous. Making the assumption that snakes somehow stopped the plague, they brought in numerous snakes to areas where the plague had hit. Sacrifices to the snakes were offered in return for protection from disease.

Both Ovid and Pliny believed that snakes were created from the marrow of the human spine. They held other beliefs about these reptiles, including the thought that snakes were repelled by plants with a high oil content and would therefore avoid clover, boxwood, and cypress.

In Scandinavian mythology, the snake is the offspring of the evil god Loki.

A snakeskin hanging in the house was thought to bring good luck. A superstition in the American South suggests that to dream of snakes brings bad luck. If you safely walked past snakes in your dream, you would overcome your enemies.

Snakes on a Rumanian doorway or Jewish temple represent protection.

In India, snakes represent endless cosmic waters.

Japanese legend says that the god of thunder and storms, Susanoo, often took the shape of a serpent. When he appeared on the earth for the first time, he came with such force from the heavens that he made a hole in the earth and went straight to the underground, where he lives still. The snake was believed to hold strong evil powers. If a snake crossed a woman's path, she was believed to be in great danger of becoming possessed.

In a Chinese legend, it is a giant snake who supports the earth on its coils; when the snake moves, earthquakes happen.

In many cultures, the snake represents the ultimate in treachery. The concept of the snake tempting man with forbidden fruit is well known in Christian mythology, but it also appears in other cultures as well.

Joseph Campbell, in *The Way of the Animal Powers,* relates the following myth from Kenya:

The Creator (Unumbotte) made a man, a woman, a snake, and an antelope. Unumbotte gave them seeds to plant, and one of these grew into a tree that grew tall and bore red fruit. Every seven days Unumbotte came to eat one of the fruits, but the man, woman, and animals were forbidden to eat them.

One day the snake asked why they should go hungry when the fruit was right there waiting to be picked, so the snake and the man and woman picked and ate the fruit. When Unumbotte returned, he asked, "Who ate the fruit?" and the man and the woman answered, "We did." Unumbotte asked, "Who told you that you could eat the fruit?" and they answered, "Snake did."

This story, so similar to the Christian story of the Garden of Eden, was developed by people who had no associations with Christian missionaries and no way of knowing the Judeo-Christian story. It is a wonderful example of the same basic myth having developed in unrelated cultures.

Snakes have long been considered a phallic symbol, and many stories and legends tell of a snake being a woman's lover. In the Freudian view, the phallus is the life-giving force. Carl Jung suggested that snakes are symbolic of man's unconscious desire to destroy himself.

In North American Indian cultures, snakes represented both good and evil. They were considered messengers between men and gods and were supposed to have the ability to bring rain. In some Native American groups, they were symbols of immortality.

An old superstition says if you ever see a snake trail, don't erase it or the angels won't protect you.

COMMON NAME: Copperhead

SCIENTIFIC NAME: *Agkistrodon contortrix*

DESCRIPTION: This snake is generally 24 to 52 inches long and has copper, brown, or pinkish coloration on the back with distinctive reddish brown crossbands (often in an hourglass shape) along the length of the body. The head is triangularly shaped; the pupils are vertical. Young are born with a bright yellow tail and are equally as venomous as adults.

HABITAT AND RANGE: Found commonly in dry woods, rocky hillsides, forest ravines, and the edges of swampy areas. Range extends throughout the East from Massachusetts to northern Florida, west to southern Iowa, south to central Texas.

Cherokee Indians called the copperhead *wa-dige-aska'li,* or "brown head." Feared and hated, it was thought to be a descendant of a great mythical serpent. Its eyes, which were unusually bright, were said to be eyes of fire.

Copperhead played an important role in the Cherokee killing-of-the-sun myth. In this myth, the sun is angry at people because they always make faces when they try to look directly at her. She begins to send such hot rays that the people died by the hundreds. The Little Men send two snakes to kill the sun—the spreading adder and the copperhead. Spreading Adder starts to spring at the sun but is blinded by the bright light and can only spit out yellow slime, as it still does today. The copperhead slinks away without doing anything.

COPPERHEAD

COMMON NAME: Garter Snake

SCIENTIFIC NAME: *Thamnophis sirtalis*

DESCRIPTION: Garter snakes are variable in color, though most are green or orangish black and have three yellowish stripes. Underneath they are greenish white or yellow. Length generally runs 20 to 26 inches, though they can grow as long as 48 inches.

HABITAT AND RANGE: Found in grasslands, gardens, parks, marshes, and woodlands. Common throughout the eastern United States and southern Canada, west to Texas, Oklahoma, and Kansas. Also found throughout the Northwest and into California.

The garter snake, or small green snake, was thought to be useful in preventing toothaches among the Cherokee Indians. They believed that the patient should hold the snake by the head and tail and press all his teeth at once down the length of the snake's body four times, taking care not to bite through the flesh.

The common name comes from the long stripes going down the length of the body, reminding some of a garter.

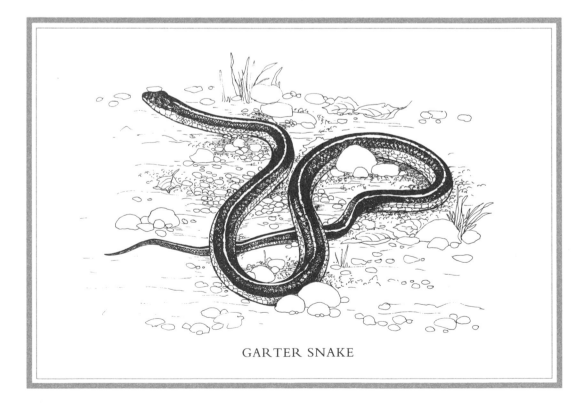

GARTER SNAKE

COMMON NAME: Kingsnake

SCIENTIFIC NAME: *Lampropeltis getulus*

DESCRIPTION: Length varies with the three main subspecies. The eastern kingsnake measures up to 82 inches, the Florida species measures up to 66 inches, and the black kingsnake measures up to 58 inches. Coloration also varies. A white chain pattern on black characterizes the eastern kingsnake; the black kingsnake is almost completely black with just traces of yellowish spots.

HABITAT AND RANGE: Commonly found in pastures, woods, or roadsides near water throughout the southern areas of the United States.

KINGSNAKE

The kingsnake is a kind of constrictor, which kills its prey by winding its body around the victim and squeezing until it suffocates. A similar species, the milk snake, *Lampropeltis triangulum*, has beautiful markings and searches for mice and other small rodents in grassy areas. Because it frequents fields where cattle graze, the superstition somehow developed that the snakes would actually rise up and drink from a cow's udder during the night, thus stealing milk from the farmer. Even today this constrictor is called a milk snake.

As the name kingsnake implies, this snake species can handle competition from most other kinds of snakes, including the rattlesnake. If the king and the rattler fight, the kingsnake seems unaffected by the venom from the rattlesnake. If the rattler happens to bite itself in the confusion of the fight, it will die from its own venom.

COMMON NAME: Rattlesnake, Western

SCIENTIFIC NAME: *Crotalus viridis*

DESCRIPTION: This snake can grow up to 57 inches in length. It has greenish gray markings with dark splotches the length of the body. The rattle is found on the tip of the tail, and two white lines are found along the sides of the head.

HABITAT AND RANGE: These are seen in prairies, grasslands, and open rocky areas. They live primarily in the Great Plains and throughout the West but can be found as far north as North Dakota and as far south as Texas.

A crested rattlesnake is often depicted with a masked shaman on Mexican pottery and figurines. It is a totem animal for certain South American Indian tribes.

The Hopi Snake Dance is performed with live rattlesnakes placed around the necks of the dancers. In spite of the potential danger, the snakes rarely bite the dancers and after the dance, they are released unharmed.

Early American settlers chose the rattlesnake as their emblem in the Revolutionary War. Flags with the motto "Don't Tread on Me" showed the rattlesnake with thirteen rattles to represent the thirteen colonies. The rattlesnake was chosen because its bright, lidless eyes represent vigilance, and while it does not seek to attack, it is fearless once it has been attacked.

According to a Cherokee myth, the rattlesnake was once a man but was changed into a snake and given rattles when it saved the human race from being burnt up by the sun. The Cherokee gave him a name that translates "he has a bell," in obvious reference to the rattle. Also called "Thunder's necklace," the rattlesnake was thought to be the most prized ornament of the thunder god.

According to legend, the rattlesnake was originally very timid and harmless and greatly abused by the other animals. Rabbit, particu-

WESTERN RATTLESNAKE

larly, picked on Rattlesnake, teasing him, tying him into knots, and throwing him around the campfire.

One day the Sun God felt sorry for Rattlesnake and gave him venom and powerful jaws but told him he must always rattle first. The next night when Rabbit began pestering Rattlesnake again, the snake rattled and bit Rabbit. Since that time, the rattlesnake has been greatly feared.

According to Native American superstition, if one dreamed of being bitten by a rattlesnake, one was treated as if actually bitten, from the belief that the body would respond physically to the dream, perhaps even years later.

The untrustworthiness of the snake is told in this Apache story of a boy who found a rattlesnake beside a path. The snake was so cold it could hardly move, but it slowly opened its mouth and squeaked, "Help me." The boy said, "If I help you, you'll bite me," and the snake said, "No, I won't. Please don't let me die."

The boy had a soft heart and hated to see any creature suffer, so he finally picked up the snake and held it close to his own body to warm it. As soon as the snake had warmed, he turned and bit the boy on the arm. The boy shouted with pain and dropped the snake crying, "You said you wouldn't bite me!" The snake slithered off into the grass saying, "That's true, but you knew I was a rattlesnake when you picked me up."

Cherokees never killed the rattlesnake unless absolutely necessary, and if forced to do this, would plead pardon from the snake's ghost. All parts of the snake—the rattle, skin, teeth, flesh, and oil—were all revered by the shaman of the tribe.

COMMON NAME: Toad, Common

SCIENTIFIC NAME: *Bufo woodhousei*

DESCRIPTION: Measuring 2 $^1/_2$ to 5 inches in length, this amphibian has a distinguishing line down the middle of the back. This species can be gray, yellowish brown, olive, or blackish above with large dark spots. Its skin is covered with warts, as opposed to the skin of frogs, which is usually smooth. Toad skin is also thick and rough, allowing the toad to stay out of water for long periods of time without drying up.

HABITAT AND RANGE: The common toad prefers sandy areas near water and breeds in the quiet waters of ponds, lakes, streams, or marshes. The common toad is found throughout most of the eastern states, with the exception of Florida, and west to Montana and Utah and south to southeastern California.

Most species of toads are named for the particular range they inhabit. For example, southwestern, Texas, western, Yosemite, and Sonoran Desert are all common names for toad species.

An Armenian folktale tells that one day a toad took a mortar and pestle and hung it around his neck and, carrying a jar of ointment, went around the countryside declaring that he was an important doctor and could cure every illness. A fox walked by and laughed. "How could you cure anything? You're simply a bundle of bumps and lumps yourself."

An Andamanese folktale explains the great drought. One day a woodpecker found sweet honeycomb in the hollow of a tree and was enjoying it when he looked down to see a toad eyeing the honey wistfully.

"Would you like some?" the woodpecker asked politely.

The toad nodded his head eagerly.

The woodpecker attached a basket to a vine and lowered it so that he could pull the toad up to the hollow. When the toad was almost to the honeycomb, the woodpecker dropped the basket, and the toad tumbled out on the ground. The woodpecker laughed, and the toad became so angry he began drinking up all the rivers and lakes until the land was parched. Although the animals begged Toad to release the water, he would not. He was so delighted with his revenge that he began to laugh and dance about, and he danced so hard that the waters spilled out of him and the land became lush once again.

Toads also played an important part in Chinese mythology. It was believed that a three-legged toad lived in the moon, each leg representing a different phase of the moon. When an eclipse occurred, it was believed that the toad swallowed the moon. In both China and Japan, toad skin is used as a source of leather.

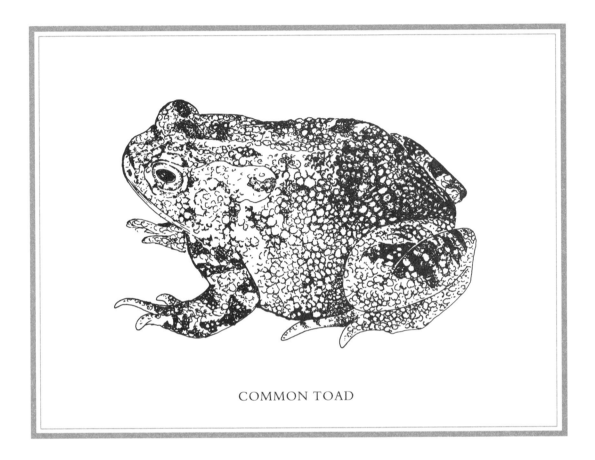

COMMON TOAD

The toad's head was thought to contain a stone that held medicinal and magical powers. Shakespeare alluded to this when he wrote, "The toad, ugly and venomous, wears yet a precious jewel in its head."

One superstition suggests that if a toad is driven into a corner, it will spit fire and fly out at you. Toads were considered friends of Satan and, in Polynesia, were symbols of death. In Mexico, the toad represented the earth.

In some rural areas, it was thought that if newlyweds saw a toad in the road, they would have a happy marriage.

COMMON NAME: Turtle, Eastern Box

SCIENTIFIC NAME: *Terrapene carolina*

DESCRIPTION: The shell of this common turtle is brown, olive, or yellow, high domed with yellow spots, and measuring 4 to 8 inches long. The head, neck, limbs, and tail can be completely enclosed within the shell due to a hinged lower shell. Eyes of males are bright red; females have yellow-brown eyes.

HABITAT AND RANGE: Box turtles are land dwellers, preferring open woodlands and fields. The eastern box turtle is found from southern New England south to central Texas and Florida.

SIMILAR SPECIES: The western box turtle (*Terrapene ornata*) measures 4 to 5 inches long and has distinctive radiating yellow lines. The range of this reptile includes the central United States from western Indiana west to southeastern Wyoming, south to Arizona, and east to Louisiana.

Many Native American peoples regarded the turtle as having strong feminine powers, due, in part, to the fact that while the turtle is a four-legged creature at home on land, it also has mastery over water. Both earth and water are powerful symbols of the feminine. The turtle as a feminine entity was part of many different cultures, including those of West Africa, Polynesia, Greece, and Rome.

In the Oglala culture, the Buffalo Ceremony prepared young girls for womanhood. During this ceremony, the girls are advised, "The turtle is a wise woman. She hears many things and says nothing." The girls are further instructed that they should protect themselves like the turtle, whose shell is like a shield, allowing no arrow to pass through.

In *Animals of the Soul*, Joseph Epes Brown quotes J. R. Walker as saying: "The symbolic basis for the representation of the turtle . . . is found in the belief that the turtle has power over the functional diseases peculiar to women, and also over conception, birth, and the period of infancy. The eating of the living heart of the turtle is regarded as a positive cure for menstrual disorders and barrenness."

Turtles were often used as amulets because they were considered difficult to kill, and this protective power was thought to transfer to the wearer of the amulet. The heart of the turtle was thought to represent strength, endurance, and longevity.

The Onondaga people of the northeastern woodlands tell this story of creation:

Before the earth was created it was only water, and the ancient chief who lived in the sky had a young wife who dreamed she saw a great and beautiful tree uprooted. The ancient chief said that, as with all important dreams, everyone must work to make the dream come true, so he, himself, found a

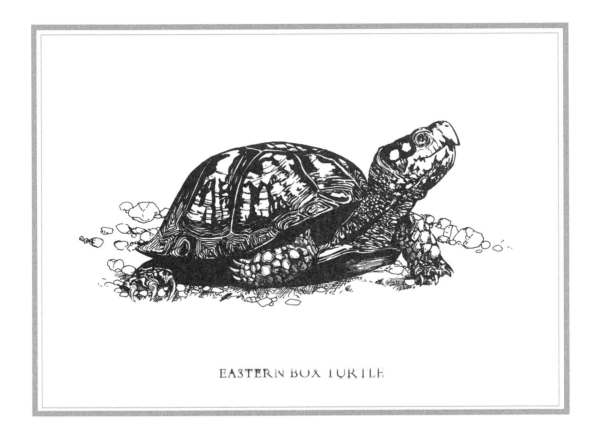

EASTERN BOX TURTLE

large tree in the sky and uprooted it. The young wife looked deep into the hole where the tree had been and suddenly lost her balance and tumbled downward. As she fell, she grabbed a handful of seeds from the tree.

The animals below saw her falling. Two swans caught her but did not know what to do with her—they knew she could not live in the water. One by one, the animals dove far beneath the water to try to bring up earth for her to stand on. All failed until a small muskrat said she would try. She dove deeper and deeper, almost dying with the effort, but at the very last she was able to grasp a handful of earth and bring it to the surface with her.

She put it on the turtle's back, and there it grew and grew and became the earth. Even today you can see the marks of the muskrat's tiny paws on the turtle's back. The Navajo say that the reason the turtle walks so slowly is because it is carrying the weight of the world on its back.

Tortoises also play an important part in various myths about the Great Flood. The Delaware Indian myth states that a giant tortoise, symbolizing earth, saved the people from the Great Flood.

According to the Winnebago Indians, the lower shell of the turtle represents the earth, the upper shell, the heavens.

Hindus also believe the turtle is an important character in creation. One Hindu myth says that the turtle supports the elephant on whose back the world sits.

In Chinese mythology, the four feet of the turtle represent the four corners of the earth. It is a water, or yin, principle and is sometimes called the Black Warrior, symbolic of strength, endurance, and longevity. In Oriental myth turtles were said to have lived to be a thousand years old.

Turtles were sometimes considered messengers between men and the god of the sea, particularly among the Ainus of Japan.

Perhaps the best-known tale of the turtle is Aesop's fable about the tortoise and the hare in which the tortoise, through perseverance, wins a foot race with the hare.

GLOSSARY

AESOP—A Greek slave born on the island of Samos in about 630 B.C. Credited with compiling a collection of fables generally conceded to be of folk origin.

AMULET—A good luck charm carried on one's body or kept in the home and thought to be protection from such situations as lightning, attacks by thieves or animals, or evil in general. Amulets are also thought to bring good luck in business, trading, and love. In America, the most common amulets are horseshoes and rabbits' feet.

FABLE—An animal tale with a moral or a short story in which animals appear as characters. Fables generally are written in two parts: the narrative, which exemplifies the moral, and the statement of the moral, which often appears at the end of the story as a proverb.

MYTH—A story that explains the origin of the earth and its inhabitants, as well as the supernatural traditions of a culture, including its gods, heroes, cultural traits, and religious beliefs.

NANABUSH—Also known as Nanabozho or Manabozho, this mythical character common among many Native North American peoples is considered a trickster-transformer culture hero in the east-central and central groups of Algonquians.

PLINY—Caius Plinius Secundus, an industrious Roman compiler of natural history, lived about A.D. 50.

PROVERB—Generally considered the wisdom of many and the wit of one, this short, terse statement suggests a course of action or passes a judgement on a situation.

SHAMAN—A man or woman thought to have supernatural powers that can cure or cause disease. Most shamans do not have formal instruction; rather, they receive their powers through visions.

TALISMAN—A charm that possesses supernatural powers. Magic caps or shoes are common talismans in fairy tales and give power to the wearer.

BIBLIOGRAPHY

Belting, Natalia M. *The Earth is on a Fish's Back, Tales of Beginnings*. New York: Holt, Rinehart and Winston, 1965.

———— Belting, Natalia M. *The Long Tailed Bear and other Indian Legends*. New York: Bobbs Merrill Co., 1961.

Blassingame, Wyatt. *The Strange Armadillo*. New York: Dodd, Mead and Co., 1983.

Breummer, Fred. *World of the Polar Bear*. Minocqua, Wis.: Northword Press, 1989.

Brown, Joseph Epes. *Animals of the Soul, Sacred Animals of the Oglala Sioux*. Rockport, Mass.: Element Rockport, 1992.

Bruchac, Joseph. *Native American Animal Stories*. Golden, Colo.: Fulcrum Publishing, 1992.

Campbell, Joseph. *The Power of Myth*. New York: Doubleday, 1988.

———— *The Way of the Animal Powers*. New York: Harper and Row, 1983.

Casey, Denise. *Black-Footed Ferrett*. New York: Dodd, Mead and Co., 1985.

Clark, Anne. *Beasts and Bawdy*. New York: Taplinger Publishing Co., 1975.

Climo, Shirley. *Someone Saw a Spider*. New York: Thomas Crowell, 1985.

Connolly, James E. *Why the Possum's Tail is Bare*. Owings Mills, Maryland: Stemmer House Publishers, Inc., 1985.

Cooper, J.C. *Symbolic and Mythological Animals*. New York: Aquarian/Thorsons, an imprint of HarperCollins Publishers, 1992.

Cowan, Lorie. *Are You Superstitious?* New York: Apex Books Princeton, 1969.

Deutsch, Babette and Avrahm Yarmolinsky. *More Tales of Faraway Folk*. New York: Harper and Row, 1963.

Dolan, Edward F. *Animal Folklore*. New York: Ivy Books, 1992.

Estés, Clarissa Pinkola. *Women Who Run With the Wolves*. New York: Ballantine Books, 1992.

Ferguson, Rosalind. *The Facts on File Dictionary of Proverbs*. New York: Facts on File Publications, 1983.

Gotch, A.E. *Mammals—Their Latin Names Explained*. Poole, U.K.: Blandford Press, 1979.

Harper and Row's Complete Field Guide to North American Wildlife, Eastern Edition. New York: Harper and Row, 1981.

Hausman, Gerald. *The Gift of the Gila Monster, Navajo Ceremonial Tales*. New York: Touchstone, 1993.

Haviland, Virginia, editor. *North American Legends*. New York: Collins, 1979.

Henisch, B.A. and H.K. *Chipmunk Portrait*. State College, Penn.: Carnation Press, 1970.

Hess, Lilo. *The Remarkable Chameleon*. New York: Charles Scribner's Sons, 1968.

Hillerman, Tony. *The Boy Who Made Dragonfly*. New York: Harper and Row Publishers, 1972.

Houghton, Patricia. *A World of Proverbs*. Poole, U.K.: Blanford Press, 1981.

Kaula, Edna Mason. *African Village Folktales*. Cleveland, Ohio: World Publishing Co., 1968.

Kennerly, Karen, editor. *Hesitant Wolf and Scrupulous Fox*. New York: Random House, 1973.

Kohn, Bernice. *Fireflies*. Englewood Cliffs, N.J.: Prentice-Hall, Inc., 1966.

Lavine, Sigmund A. *Wonders of Coyotes*. New York: Dodd, Mead and Co., 1984.

Leach, Maria, editor. *Funk and Wagnalls Standard Dictionary of Folklore, Mythology and Legend*. New York: Funk and Wagnalls, 1950.

———*Wonders of Woodchucks*. New York: Dodd, Mead and Co., 1984.

——— *Funk and Wagnalls Standard Dictionary of Folklore, Mythology and Legend*. New York: Funk and Wagnalls, 1950.

Leach, Maria. *How the People Sang the Mountains Up*. New York: Viking Press, 1967.

Marriott, Alice and Carol K. Rachlin. *American Indian Mythology*. New York: Thomas Y. Crowell Co., 1968.

McDermott, Gerald. *Anasi the Spider*. New York: Holt, Rinehart and Winston, 1972.

Mercatante, Anthony S. *Zoo of the Gods*. New York: Harper and Row, Publishers, 1974.

Milne, Lorus and Margery. *The Audubon Field Guide to North American Insects and Spiders*. Chanticleer Press Edition. New York: Alfred A. Knopf, 1980.

Mooney, James. *Myths of the Cherokees and Sacred Formulas of the Cherokees*. Nashville, Tenn.: Booksellers Publishers, 1982.

Nunes, Susan. *Tiddalick the Frog*. New York: Antheneum, 1989.

Parker, Langloh. *Australian Legendary Tales*. New York: Viking Press, 1966.

Ramsey, Jarold, editor. *Coyote Was Going There: Indian Literature of the Oregon Country*. Seattle: University of Washington Press, 1977.

Sanders, Barry and Paul Shepard. *The Sacred Paw*. New York: Viking Press, 1985.

Scheer, George F., editor. *Cherokee Animal Tales*. New York: Holiday House, 1968.

Schon, Gunter. *Animals, Birds and Fishes on Coins*. New York: Sterling Publishing, 1971.

Simon, Hilda. *Snakes, the Facts and the Folhlore*. New York: Viking Press, 1973.

Wesley, Addison. *The Magic Horns: Folk Tales from Africa*. Reading, Mass.: Addison-Wesley, 1976.

Wolkstein, Diane. *Squirrel's Song*. New York: Alfred A. Knopf, 1976.

Wootton, Anthony. *Animal Folklore, Myth and Legend*. Poole, U.K.: Blandford Press, 1986.

INDEX

ABOUT THE AUTHOR

A recognized authority on nature and gardening, LAURA C. MARTIN is the author of *The Wildflower Meadow Book, Wildflower Folklore, Garden Flower Folklore, The Folklore of Trees and Shrubs,* and *The Folklore of Birds,* all published by Globe Pequot, and *A History of Southern Gardens* and *Handmade Crafts from a Country Garden,* both by Abbeville Press. She presents lectures and workshops throughout the United States on meadow gardening, wildflowers, and the history of gardens, and her weekly gardening column has appeared in the Atlanta Journal-Constitution for eight years. Ms. Martin lives with her son and daughter in Atlanta, Georgia, where she gardens, writes, and teaches karate.

ALSO OF INTEREST
FROM THE GLOBE PEQUOT PRESS

The World of Birds $15.95
"A highly readable book for bird watchers . . ."
—BIRD WATCHERS DIGEST

**Marine Wildlife of Puget Sound, the San Juans,
and the Strait of Georgia $14.95**
"The very model of a field guide"
—AUDUBON MAGAZINE

Birding for the Amateur Naturalist $8.95
"One of the best basic bird watcher books in some time"
—ALA BOOKLIST

Private Lives of Garden Birds $12.95
Wonderfully readable and popular book about bird behavior

Behavior and Learning of Animal Babies $18.95
"Delightful experience for lovers of nature and animals"
—BOOKLIST

OTHER BOOKS IN THIS SERIES:

Wildflower Folklore $16.95
Legends and stories of 105 North American wildflowers

Garden Flower Folklore $19.95
A valuable and fascinating botanical reference

The Folklore of Trees and Shrubs $24.95
"Presents over a 100 species in clear, informative style"
—LIBRARY JOURNAL

The Folklore of Birds $24.95
Beautiful, accurate illustrations; a wealth of folkore

Available from your bookstore or directly from the publisher. For a free catalogue
or to place an order, call toll-free 24 hours a day 1–800–243–0495,
fax toll-free 1–800–820–2329, or write to The Globe Pequot Press, P.O. Box 833,
Old Saybrook, Connecticut 06475-0833.